This coloring book belong to:

_____

NOEMIN.

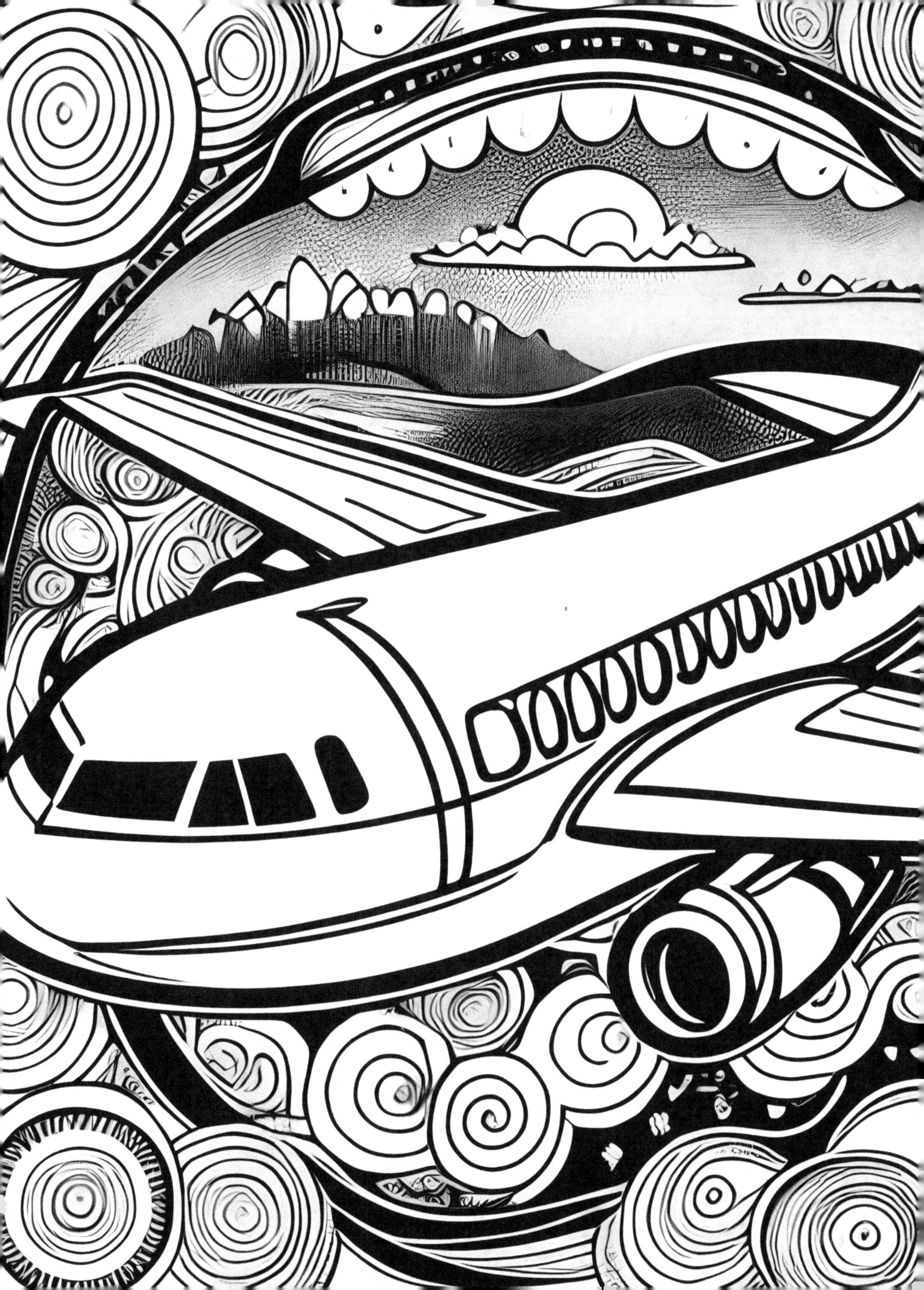

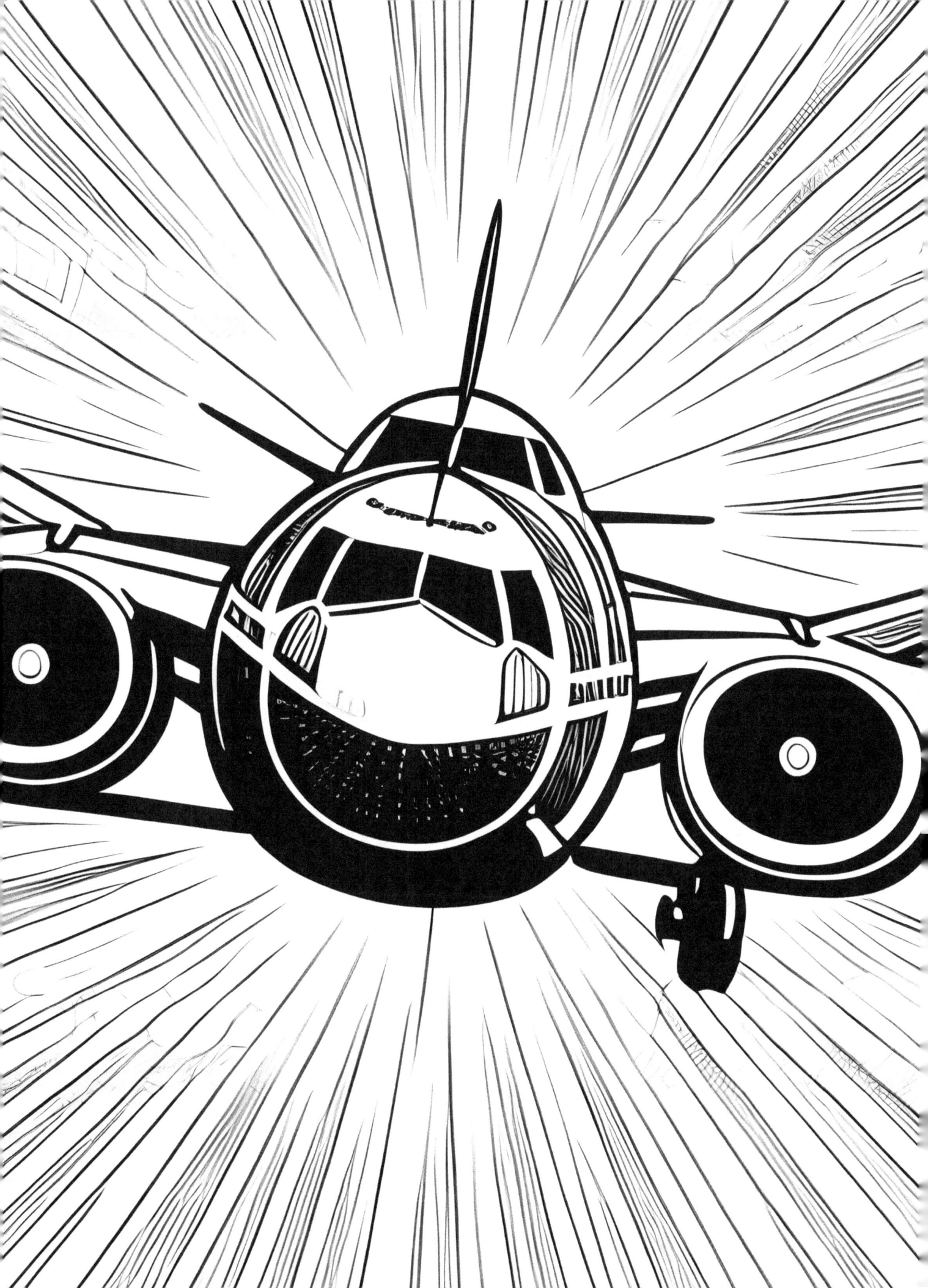

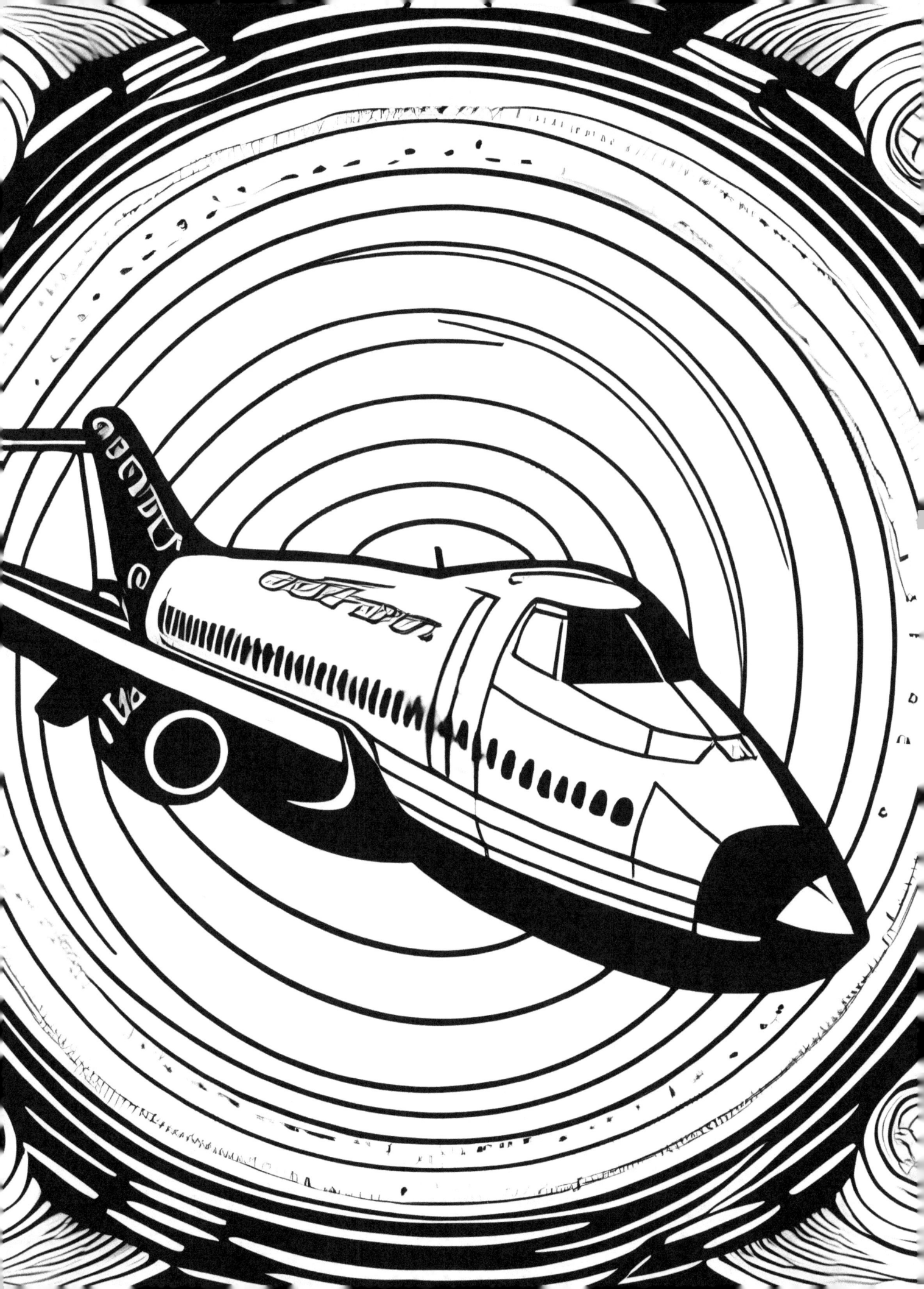

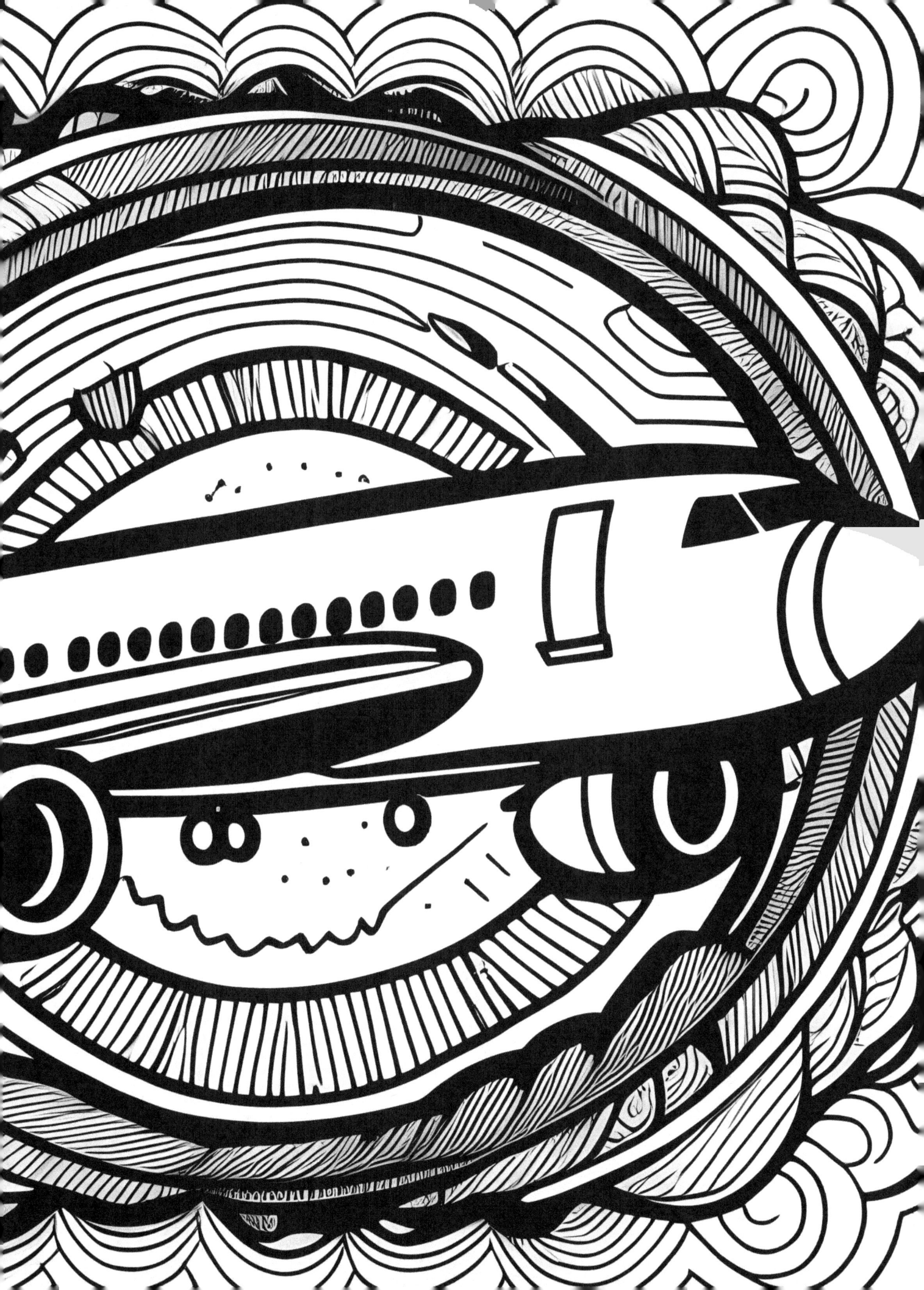

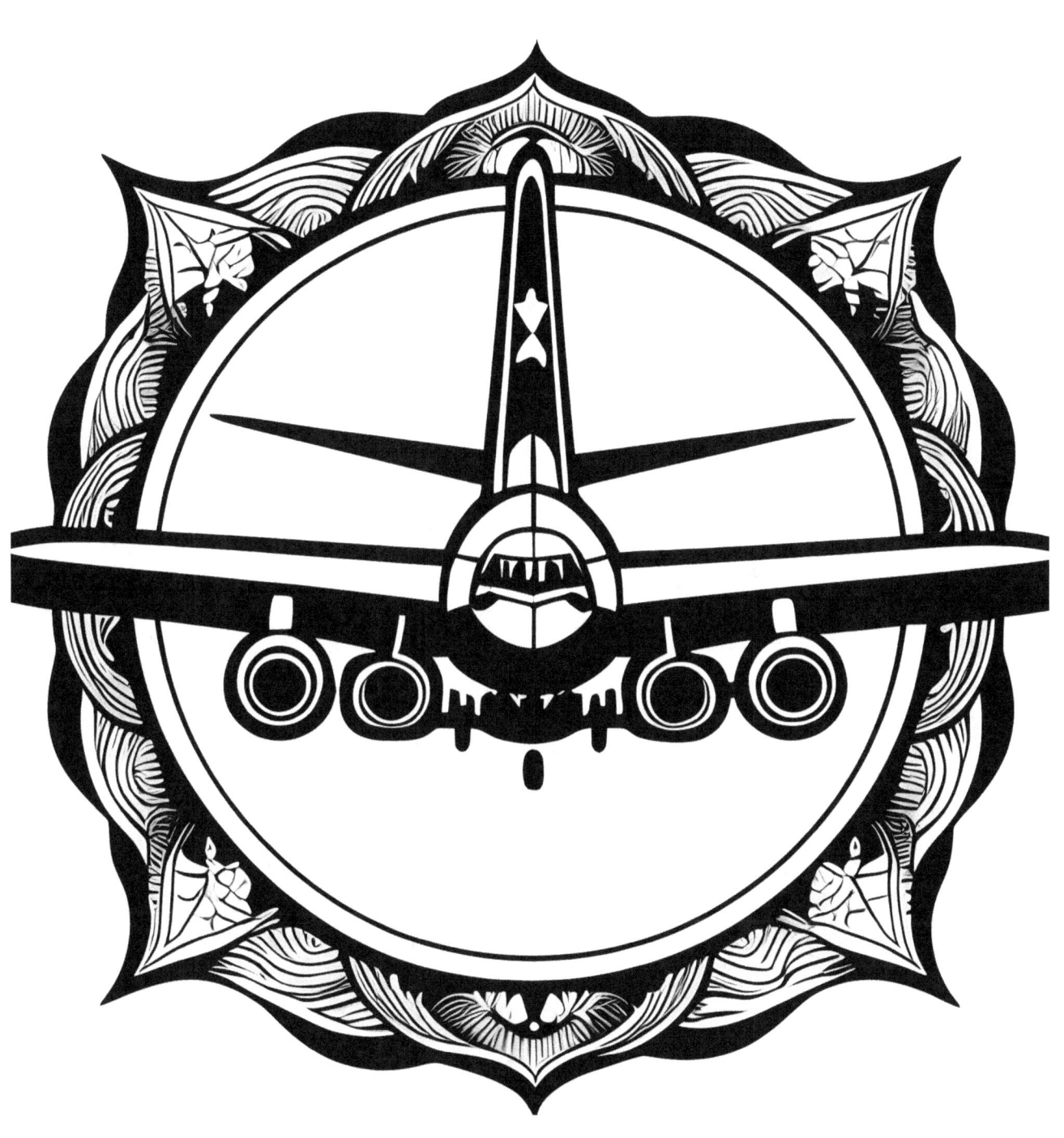

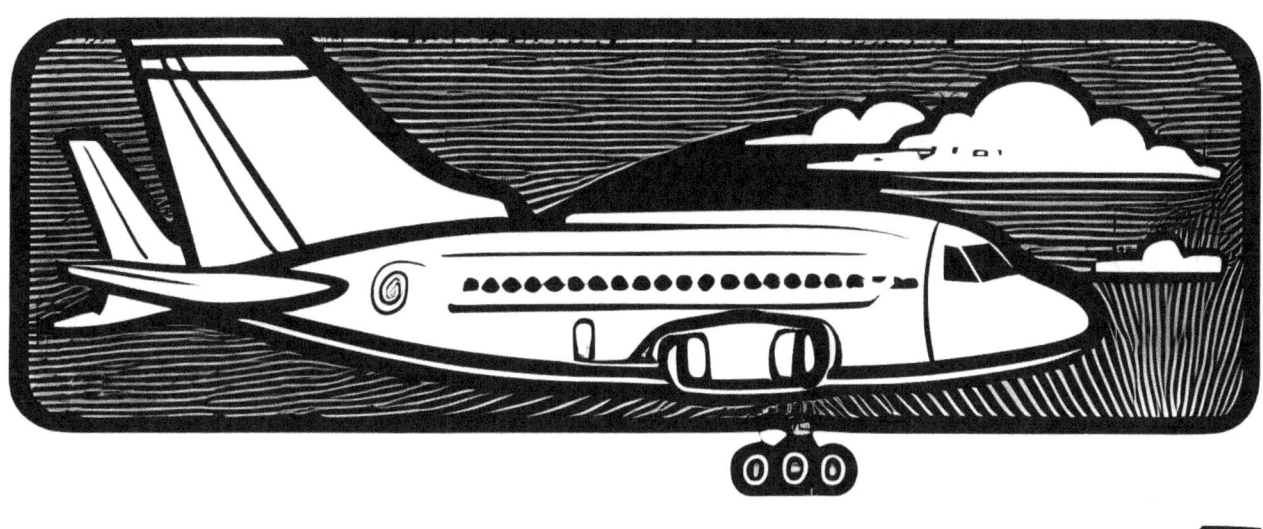

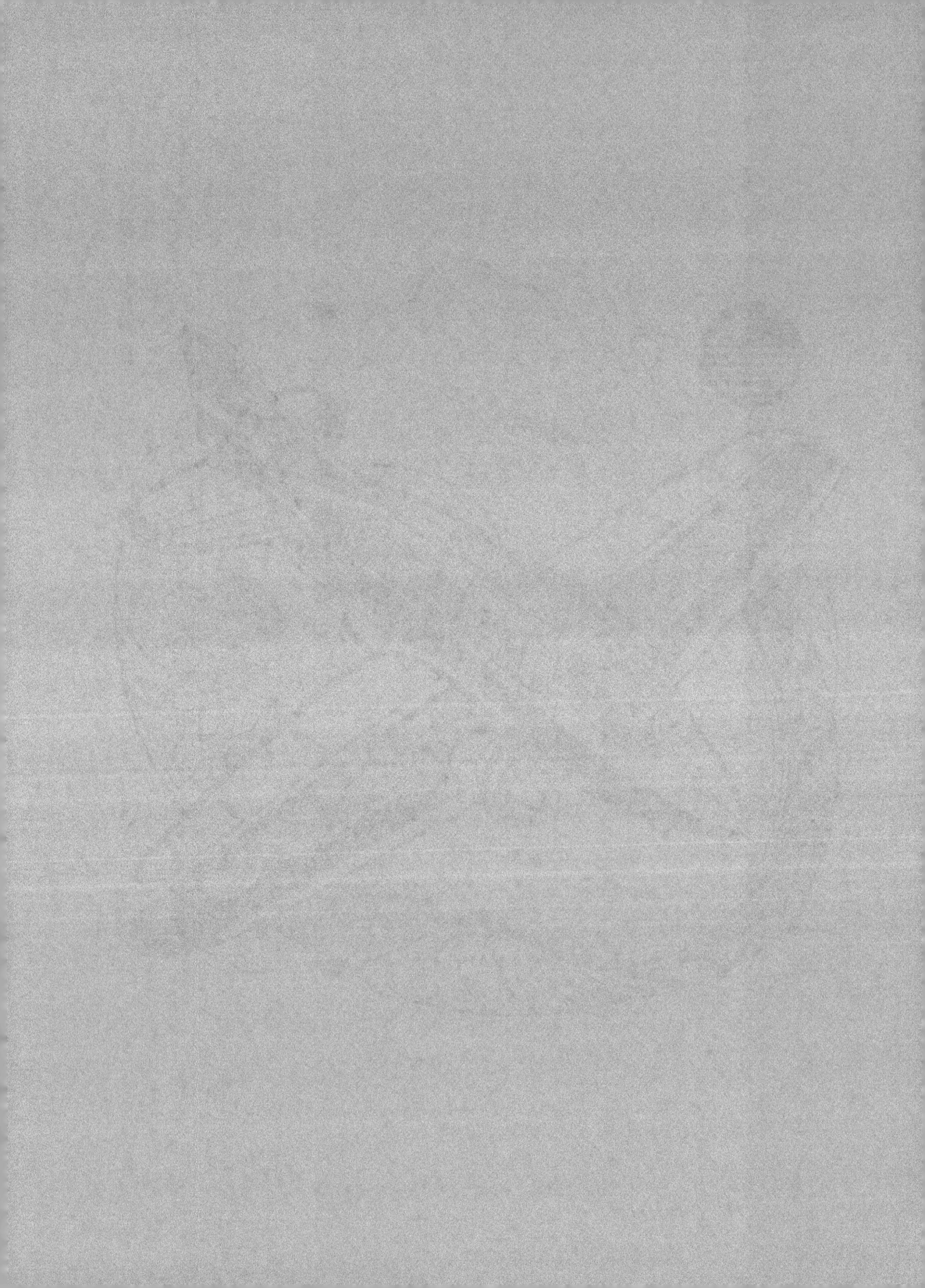

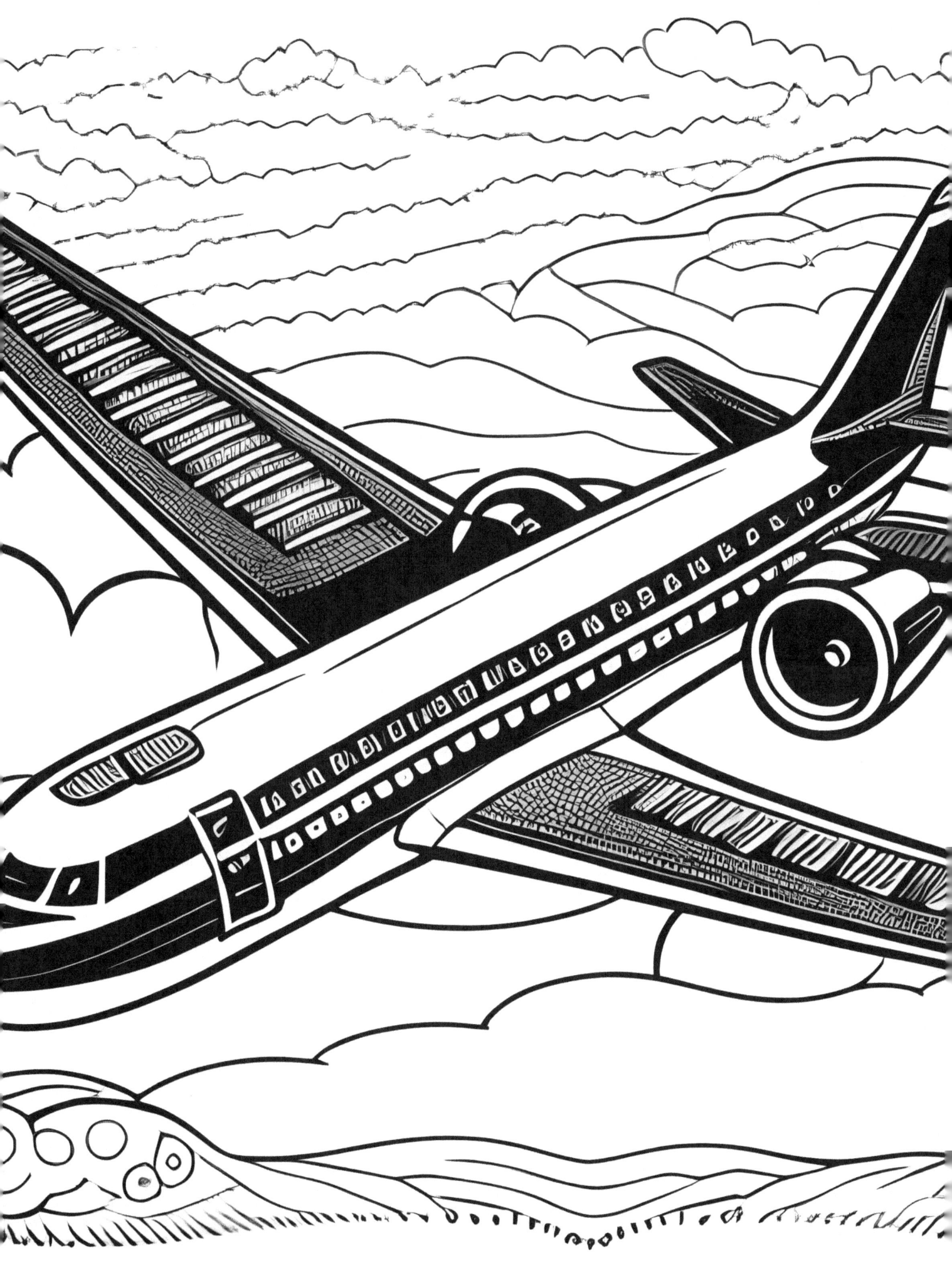

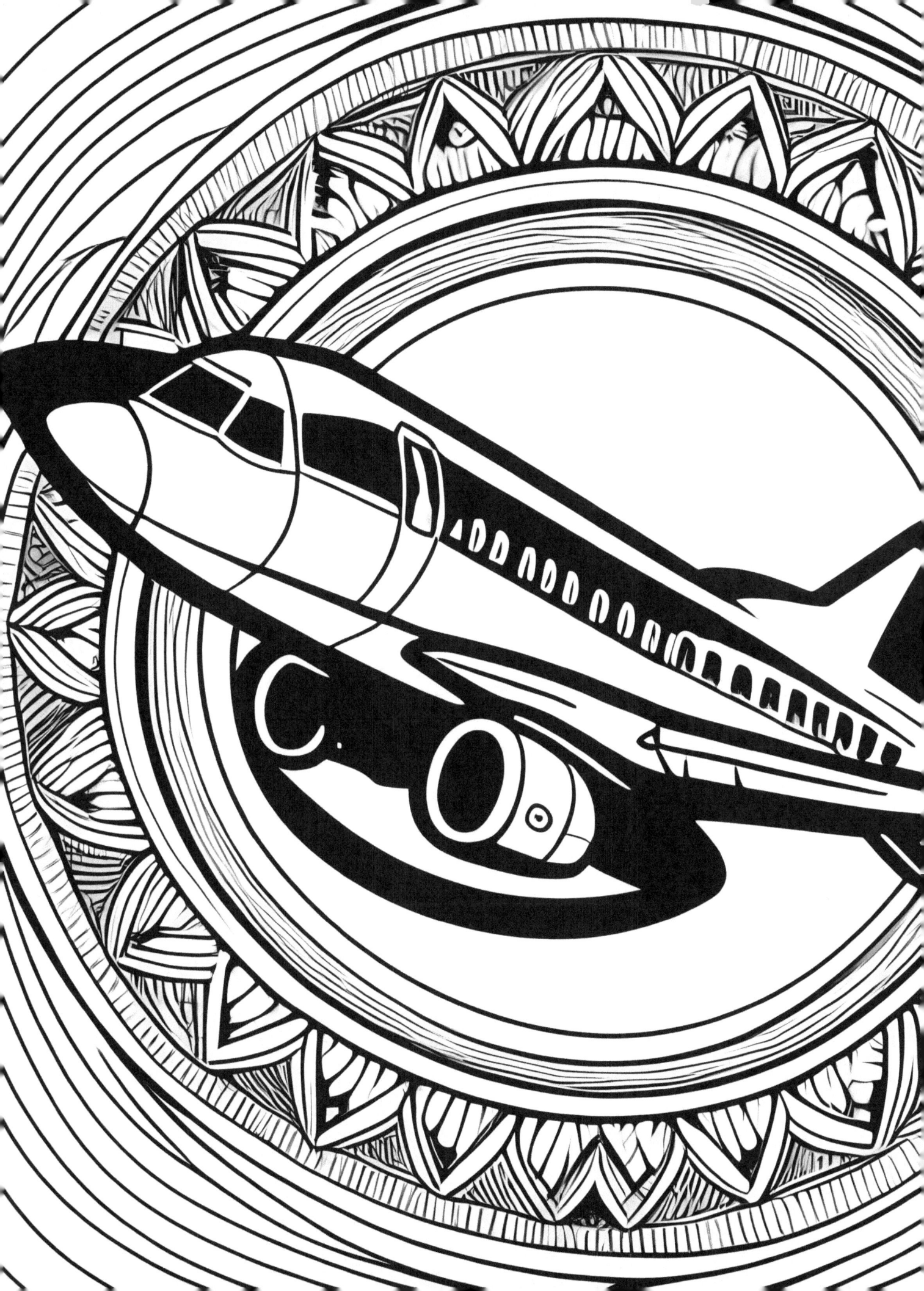

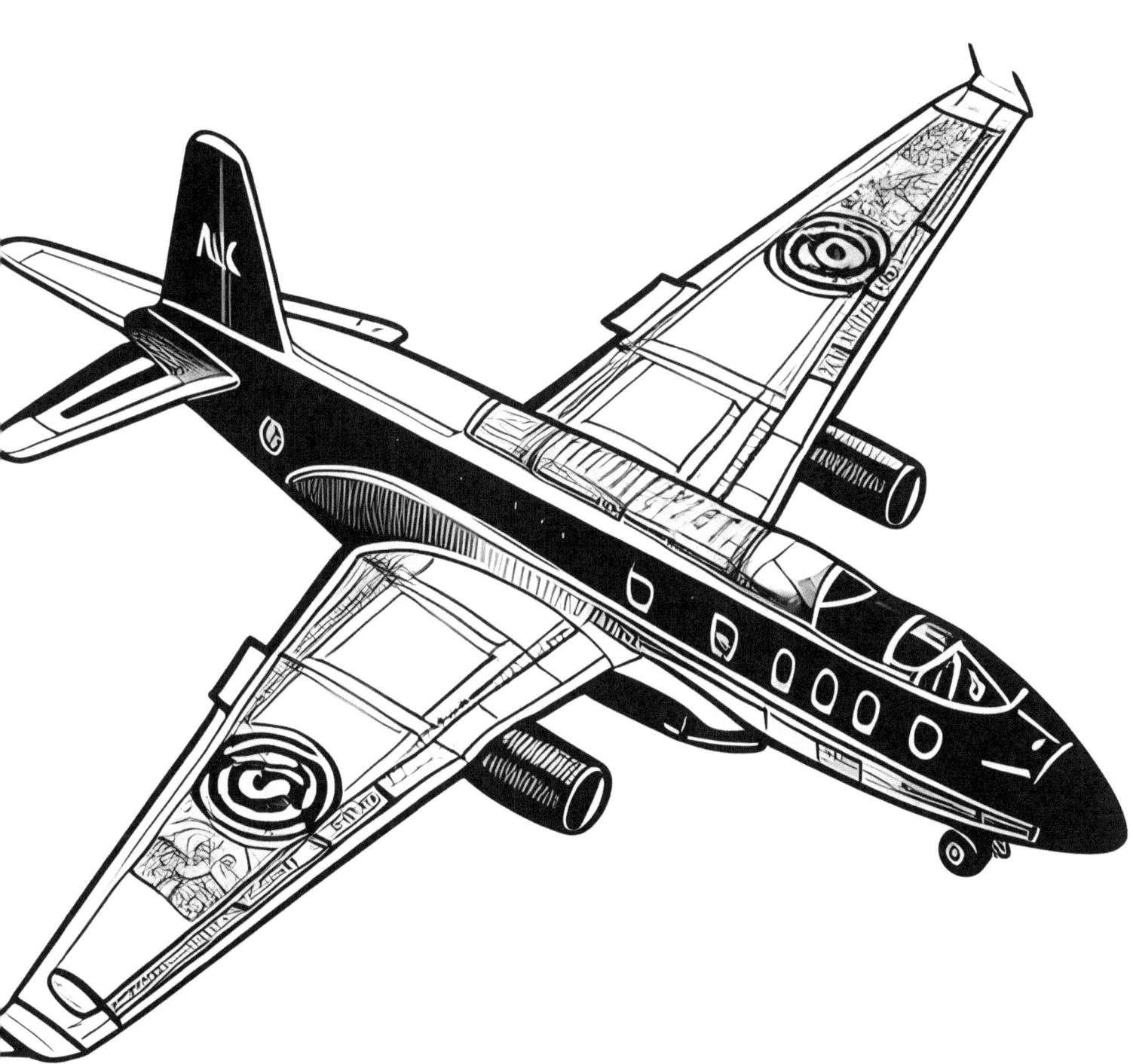

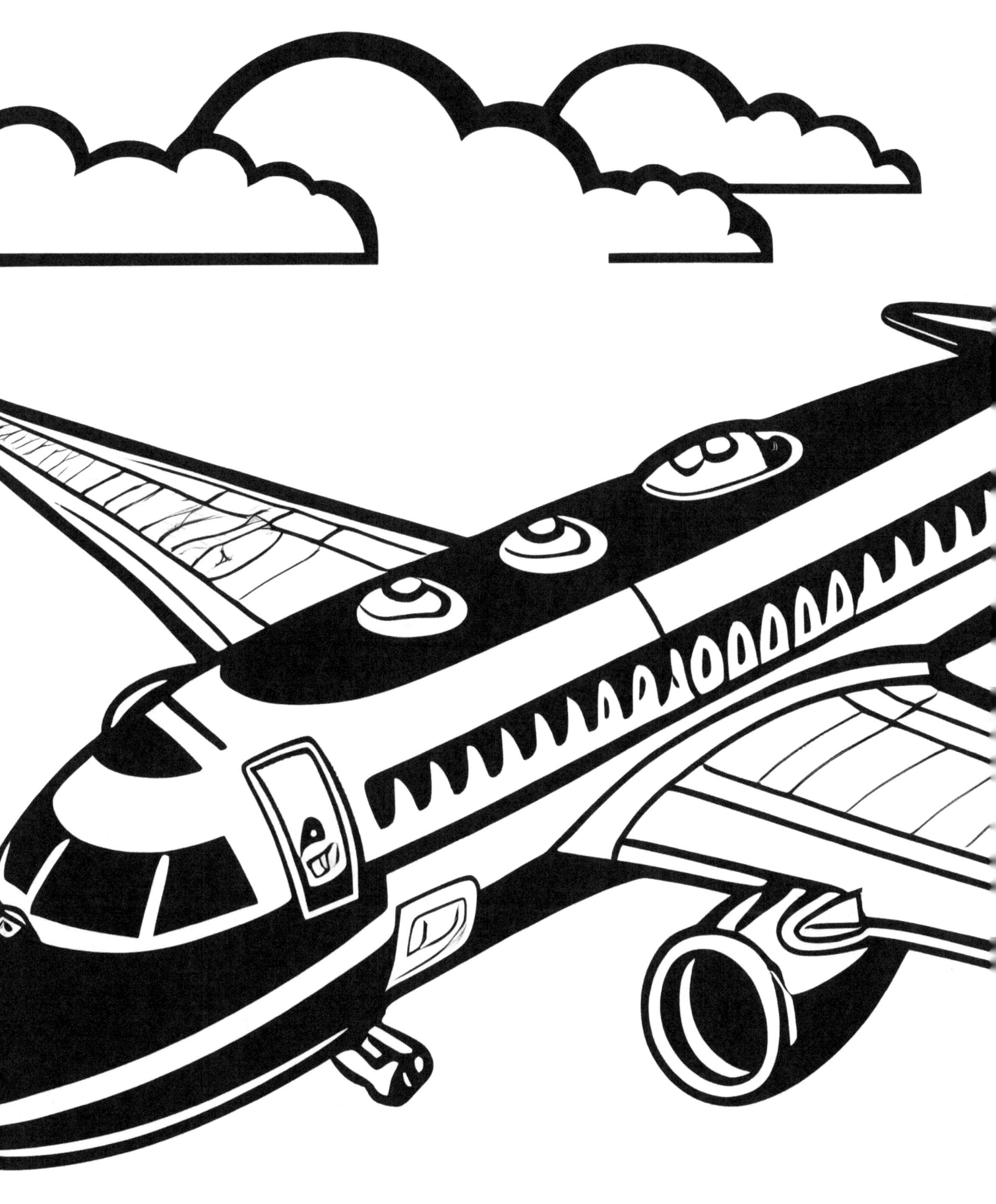

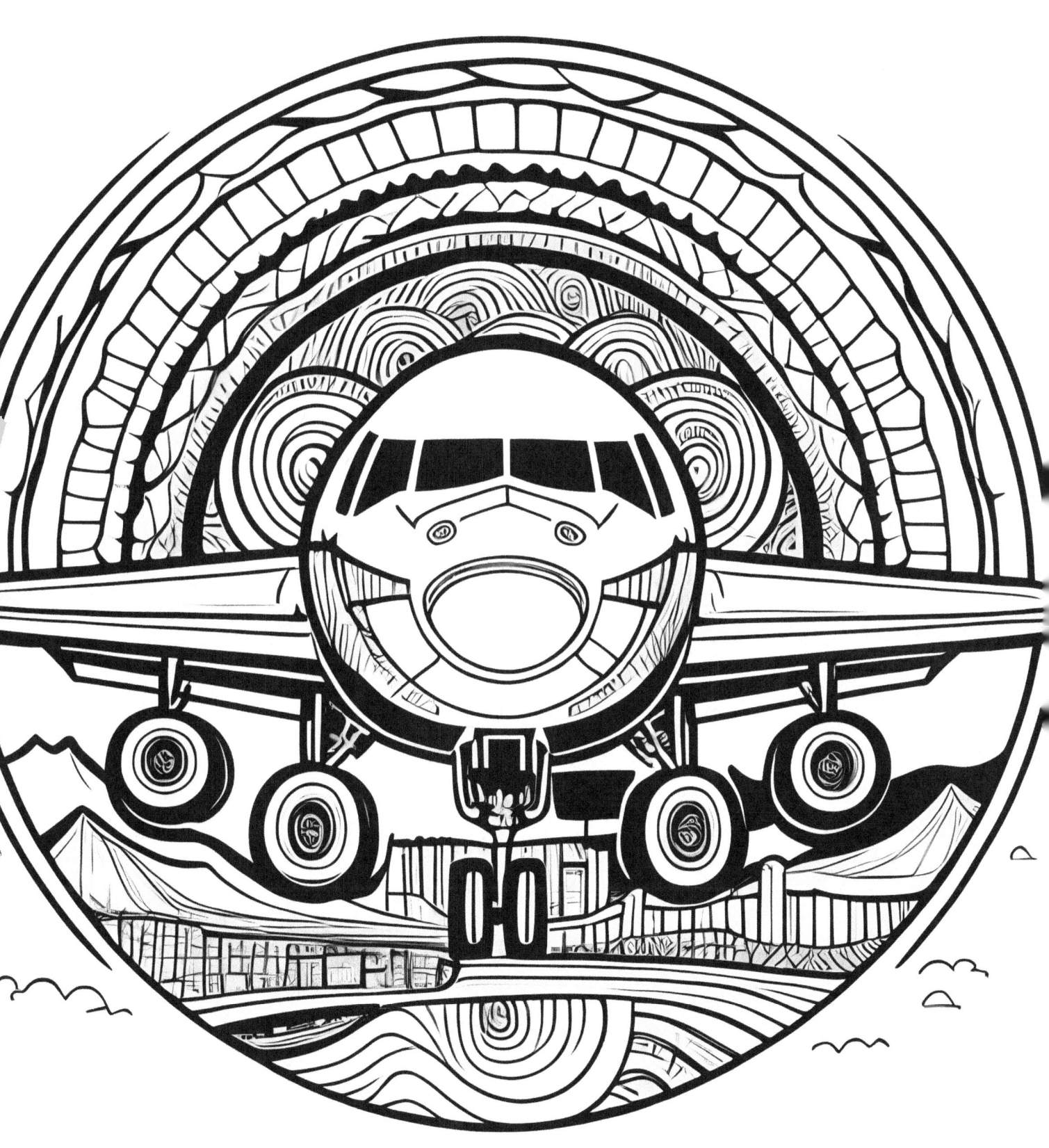

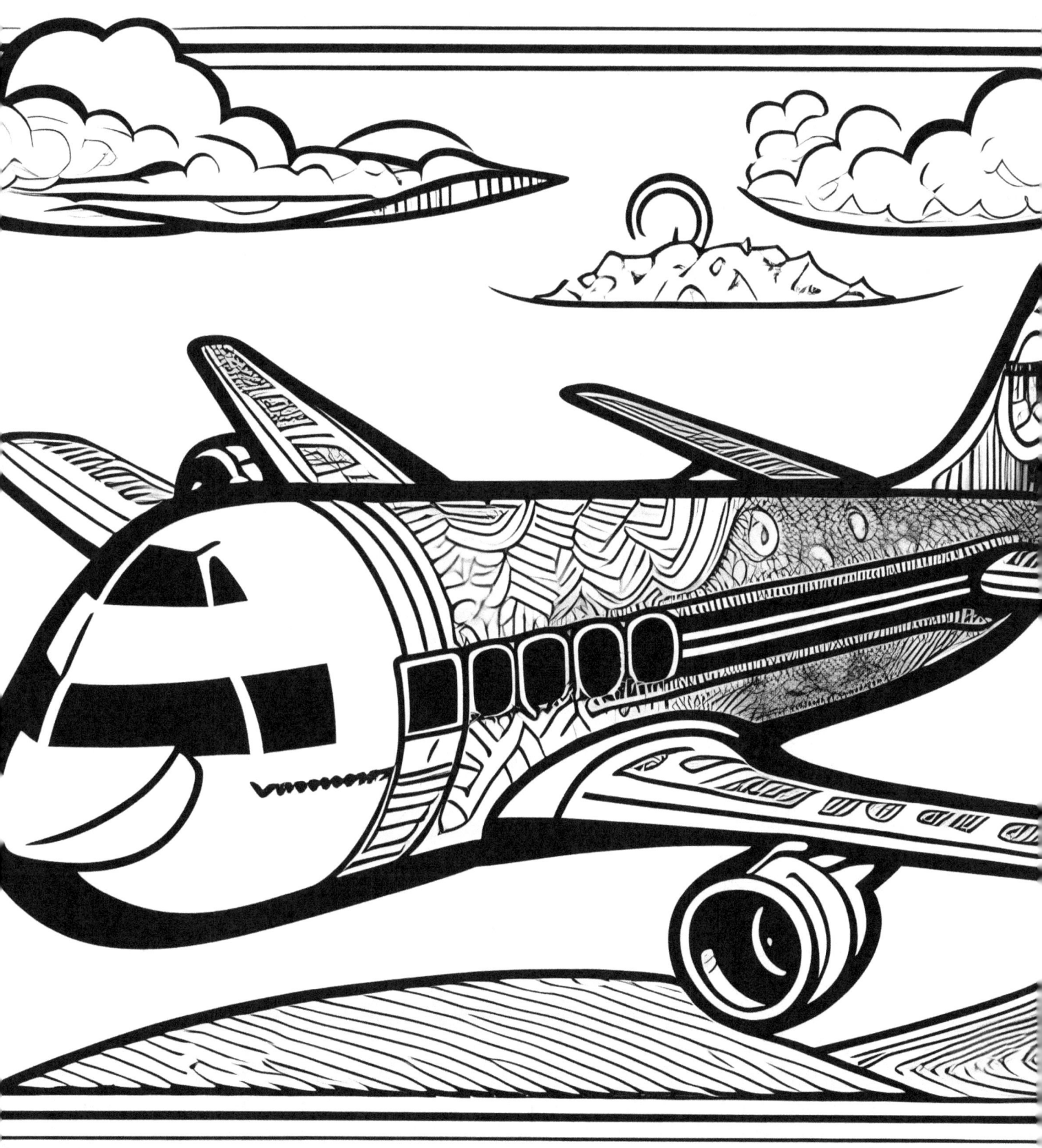

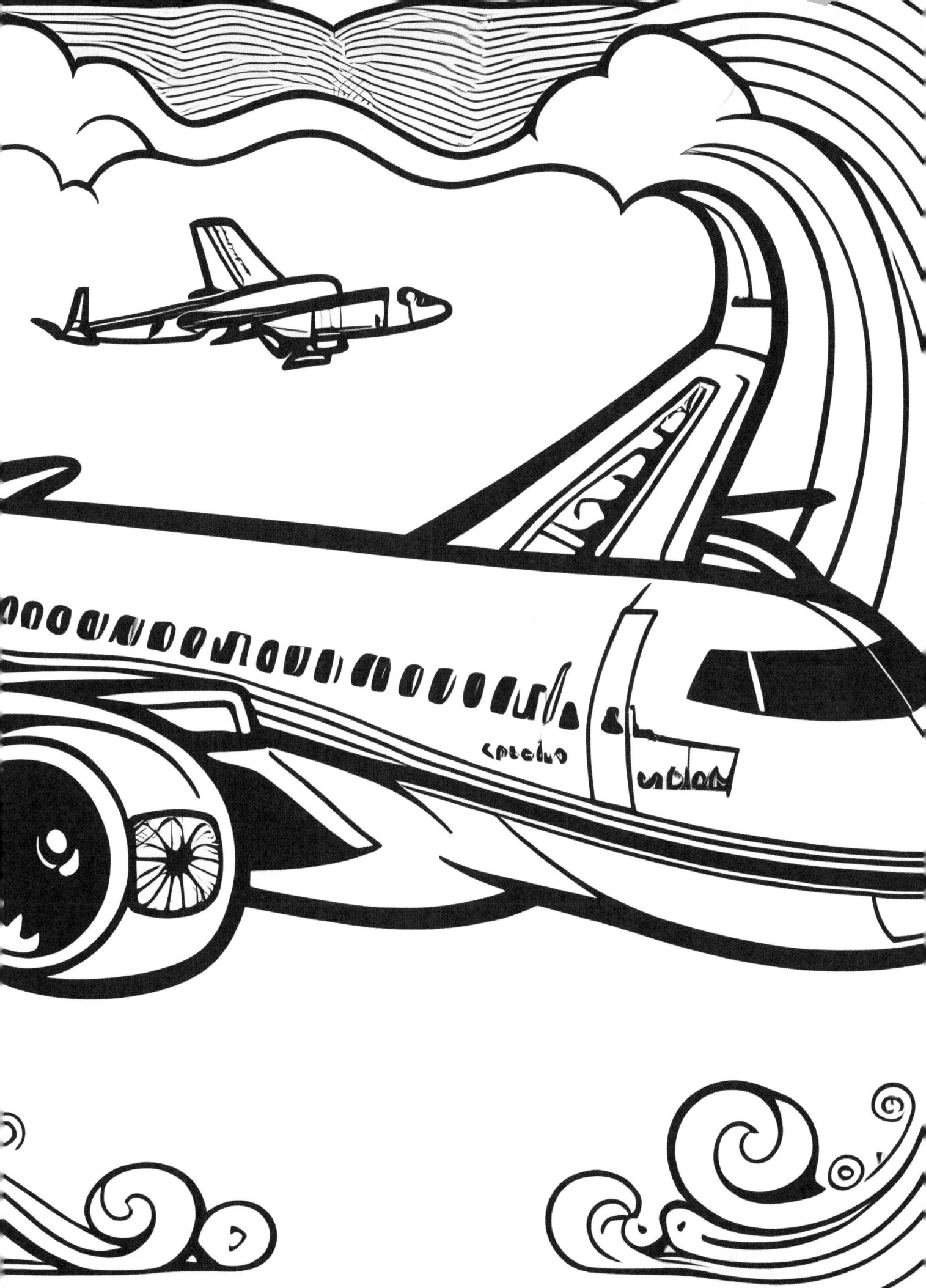

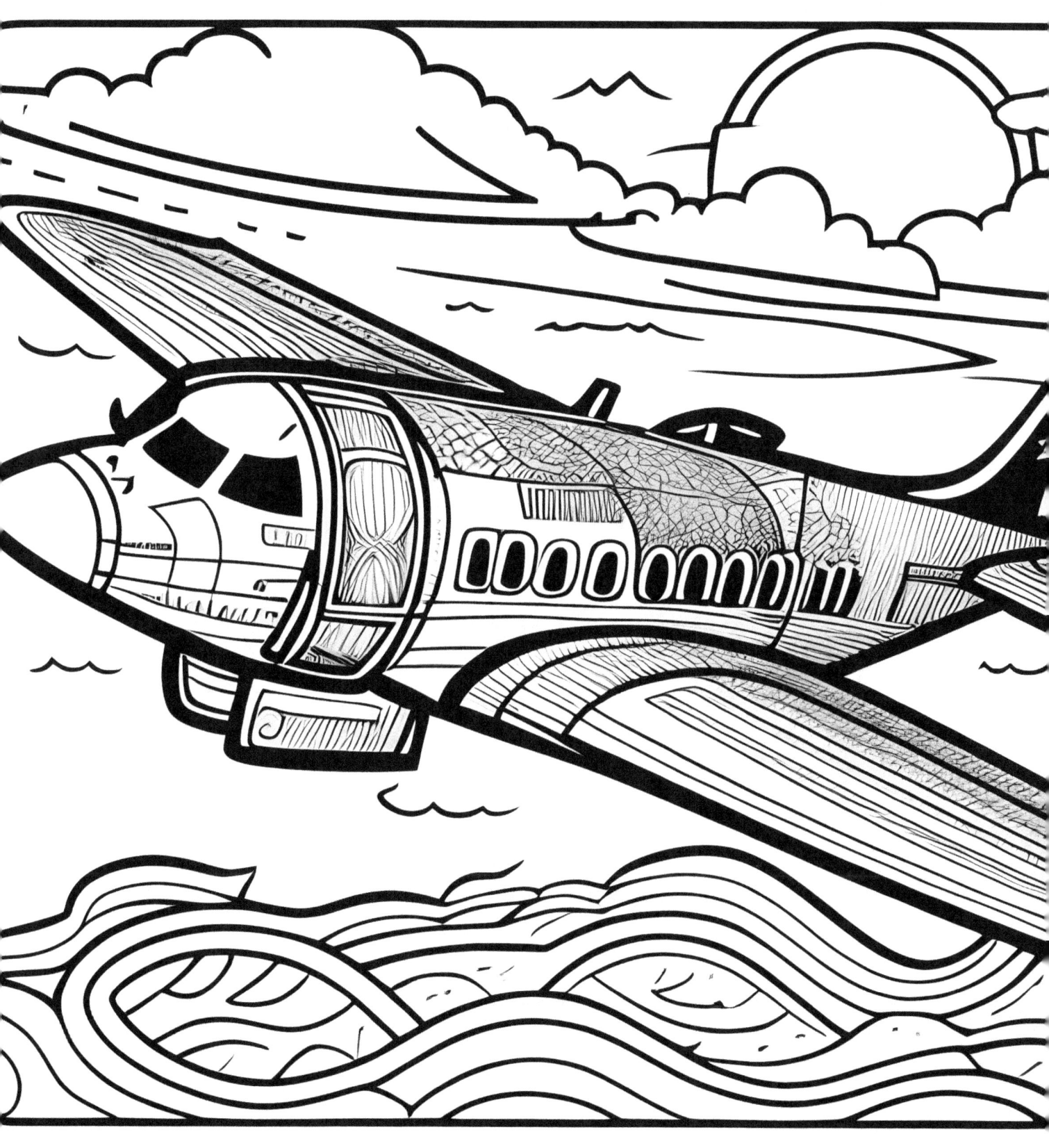

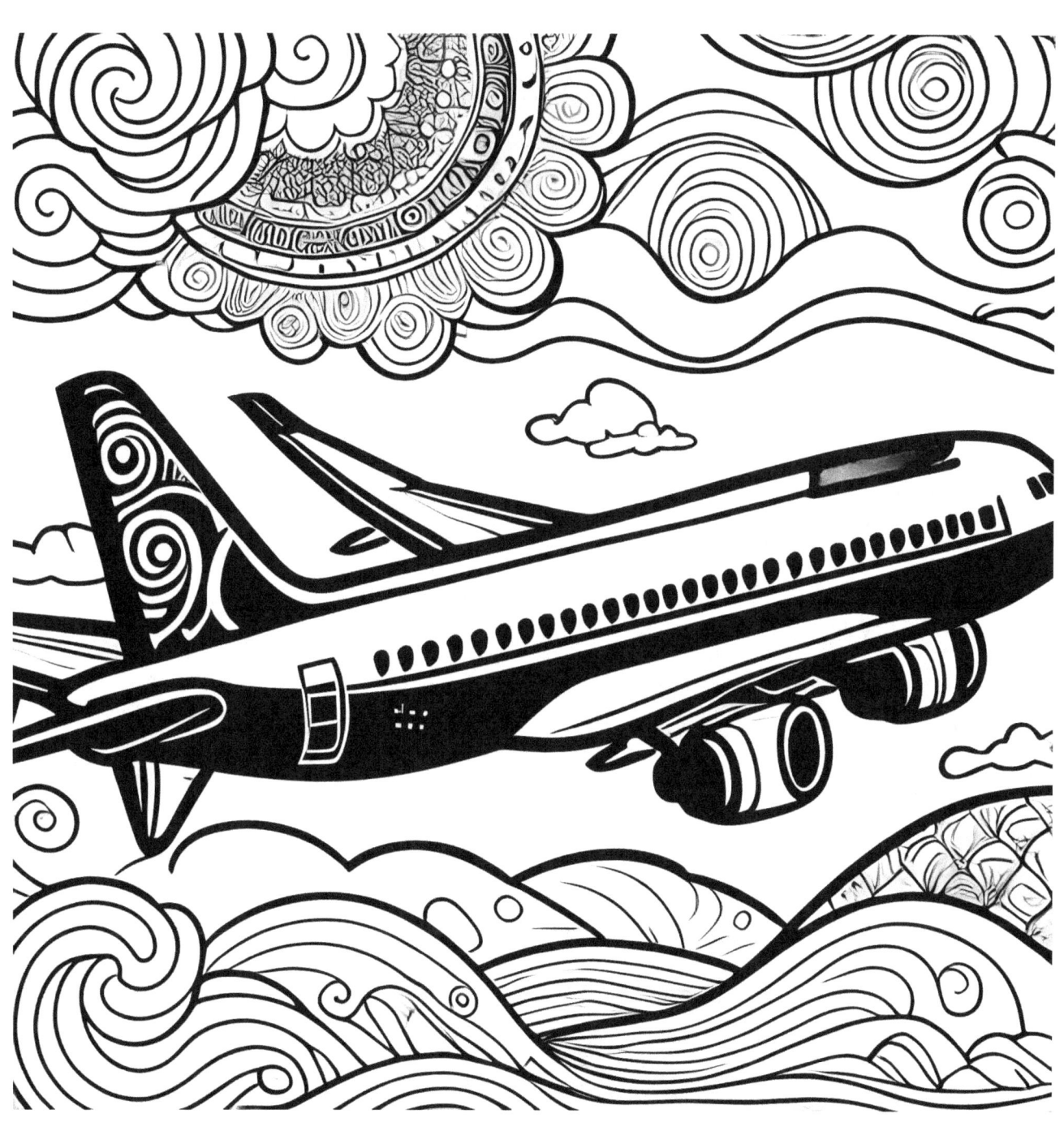

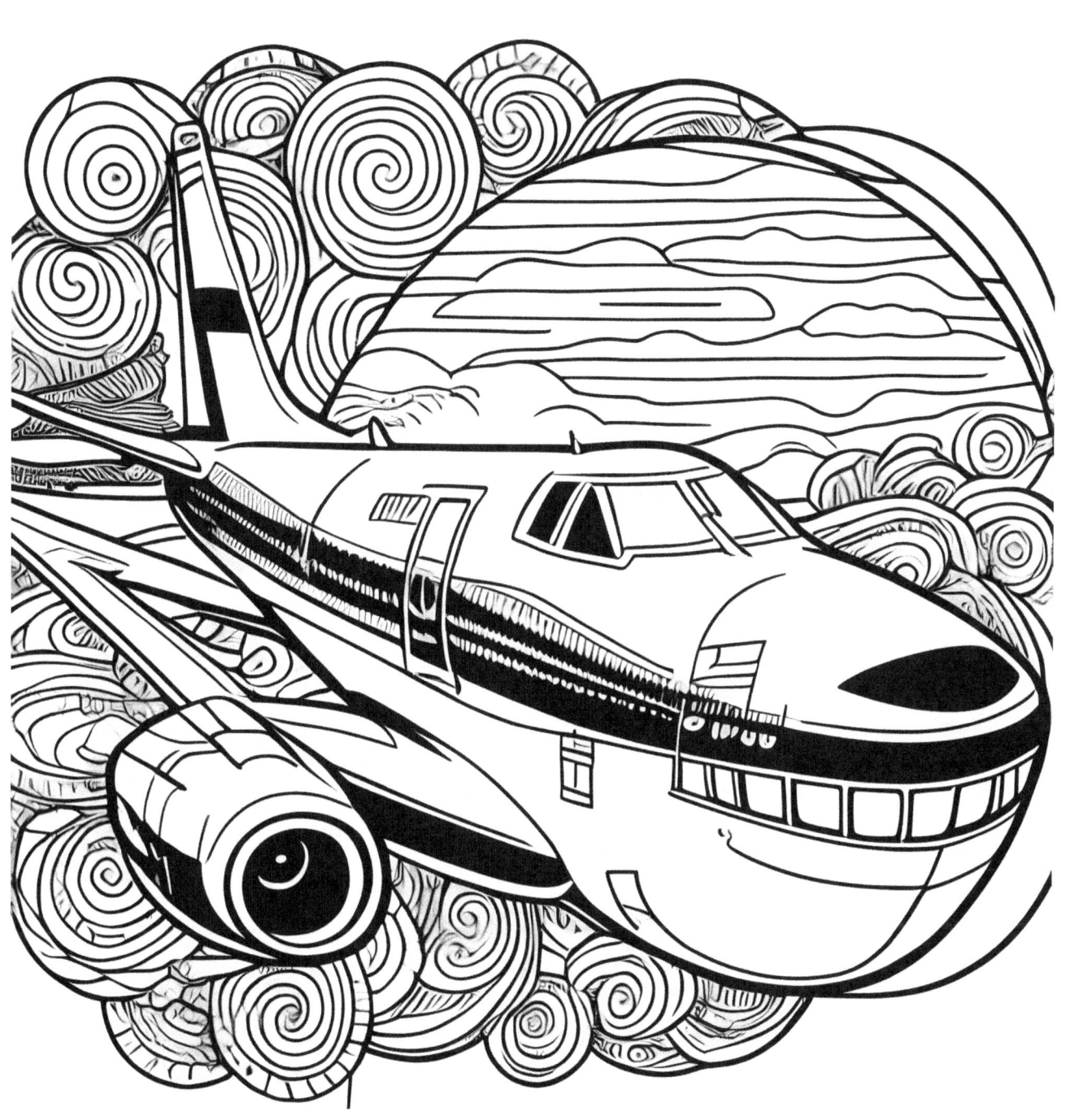

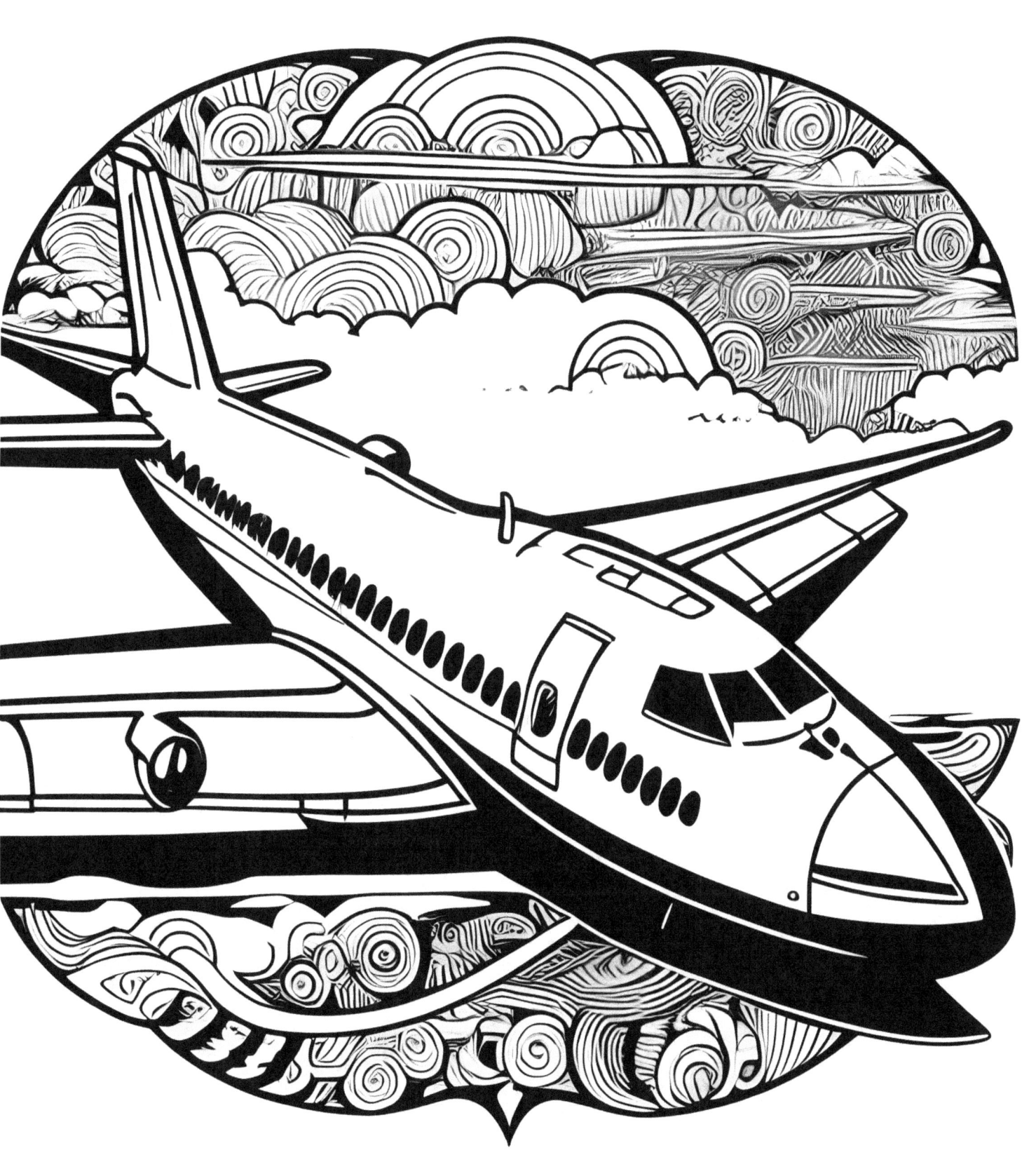

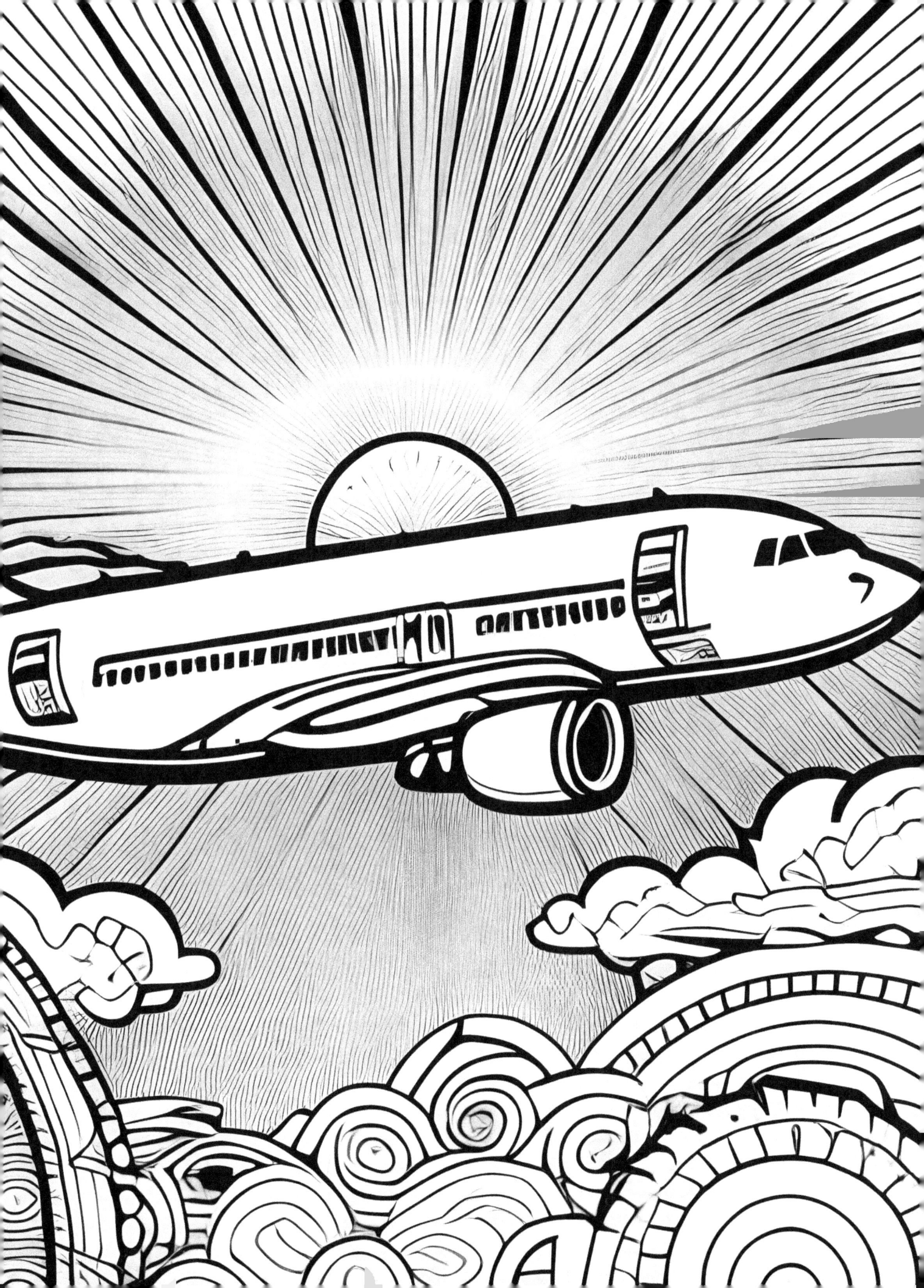

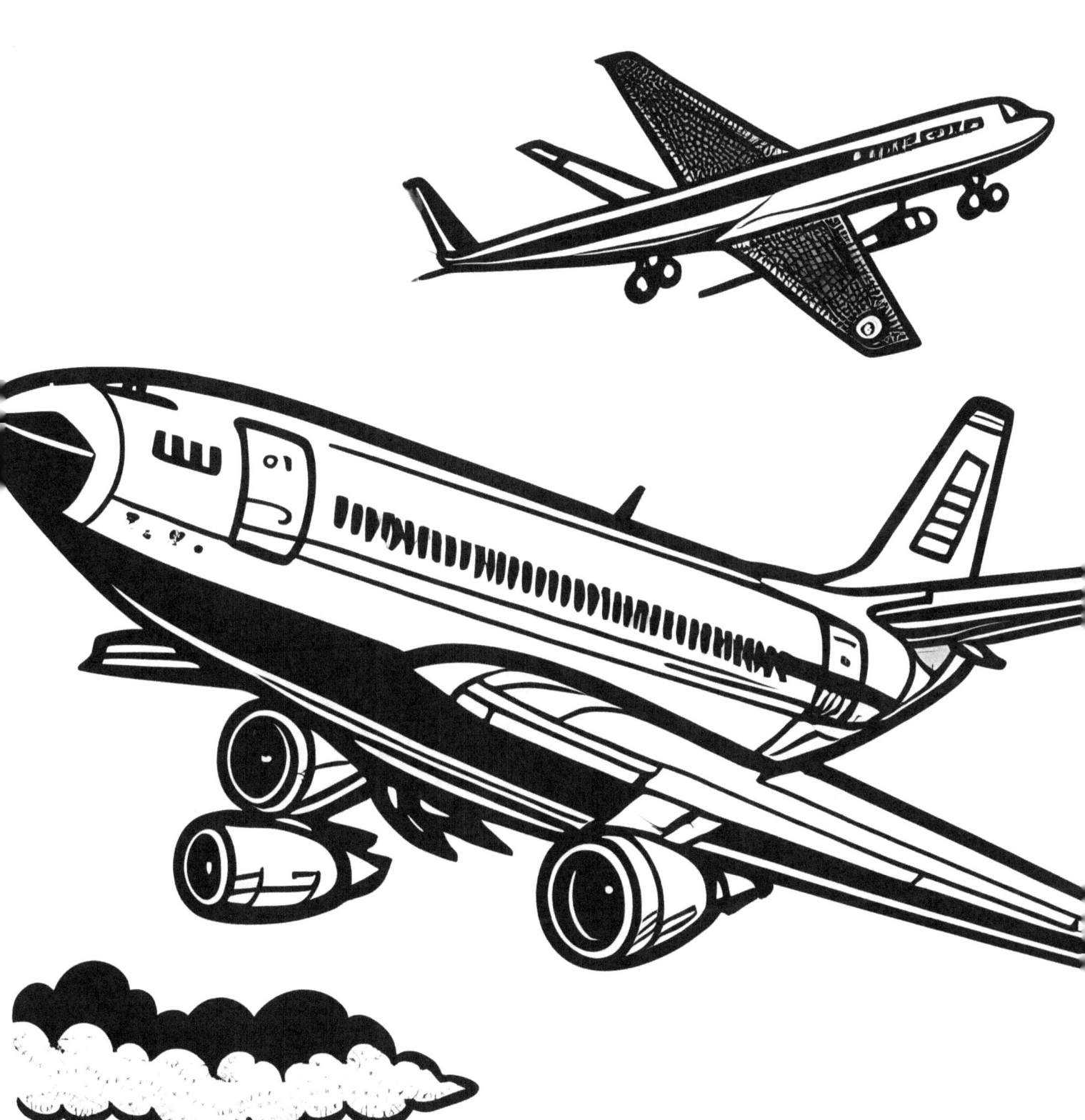

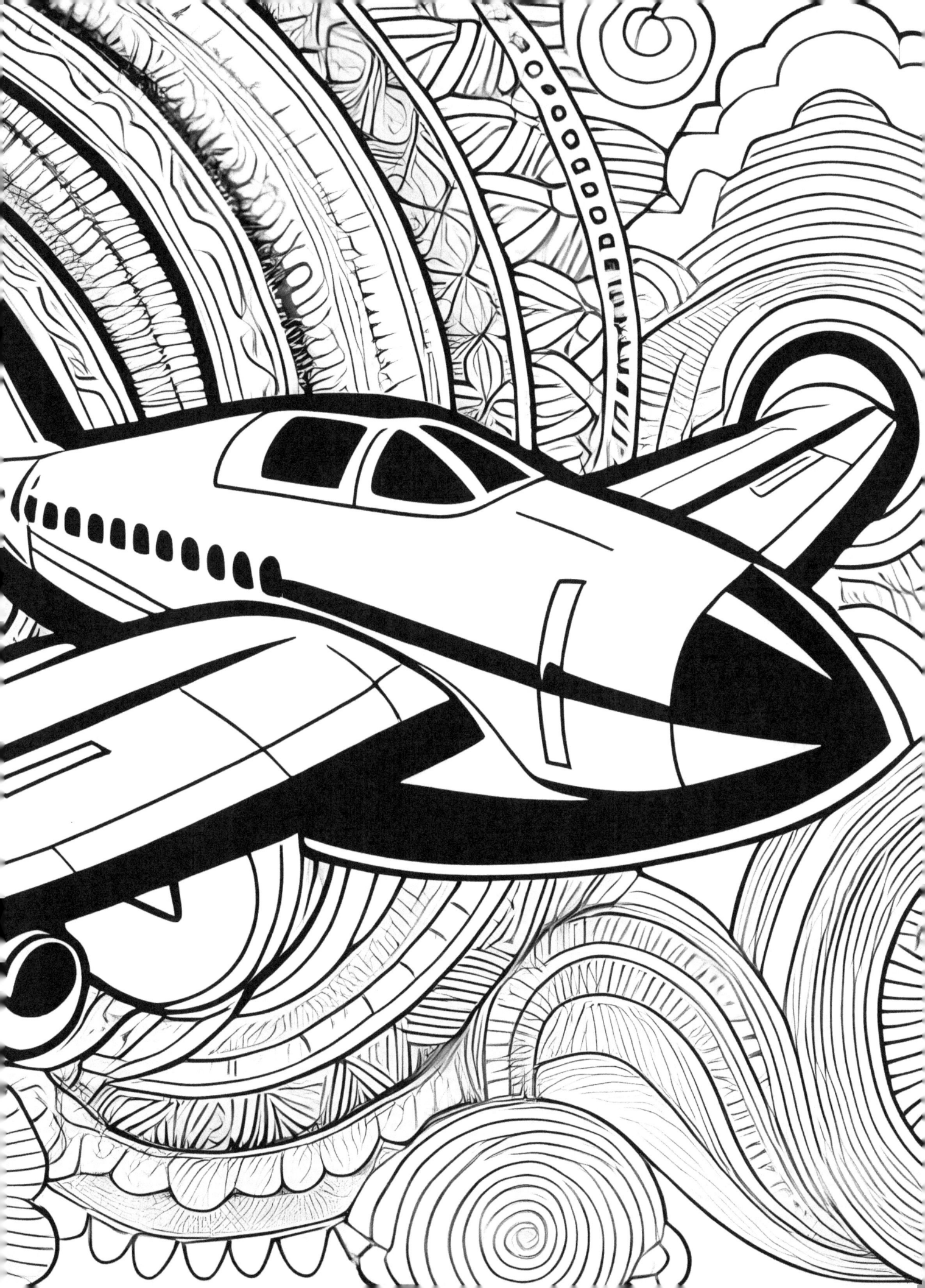

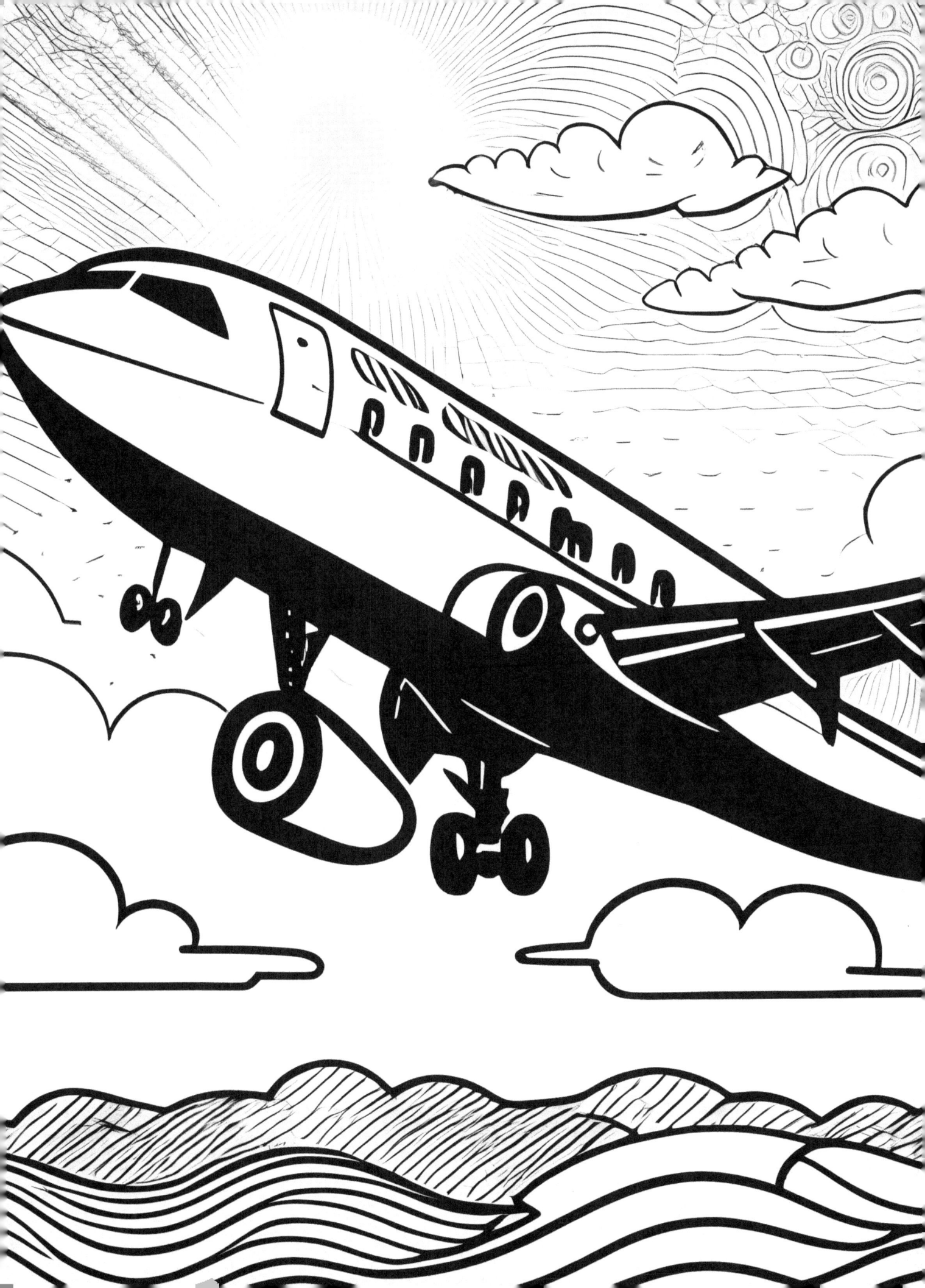

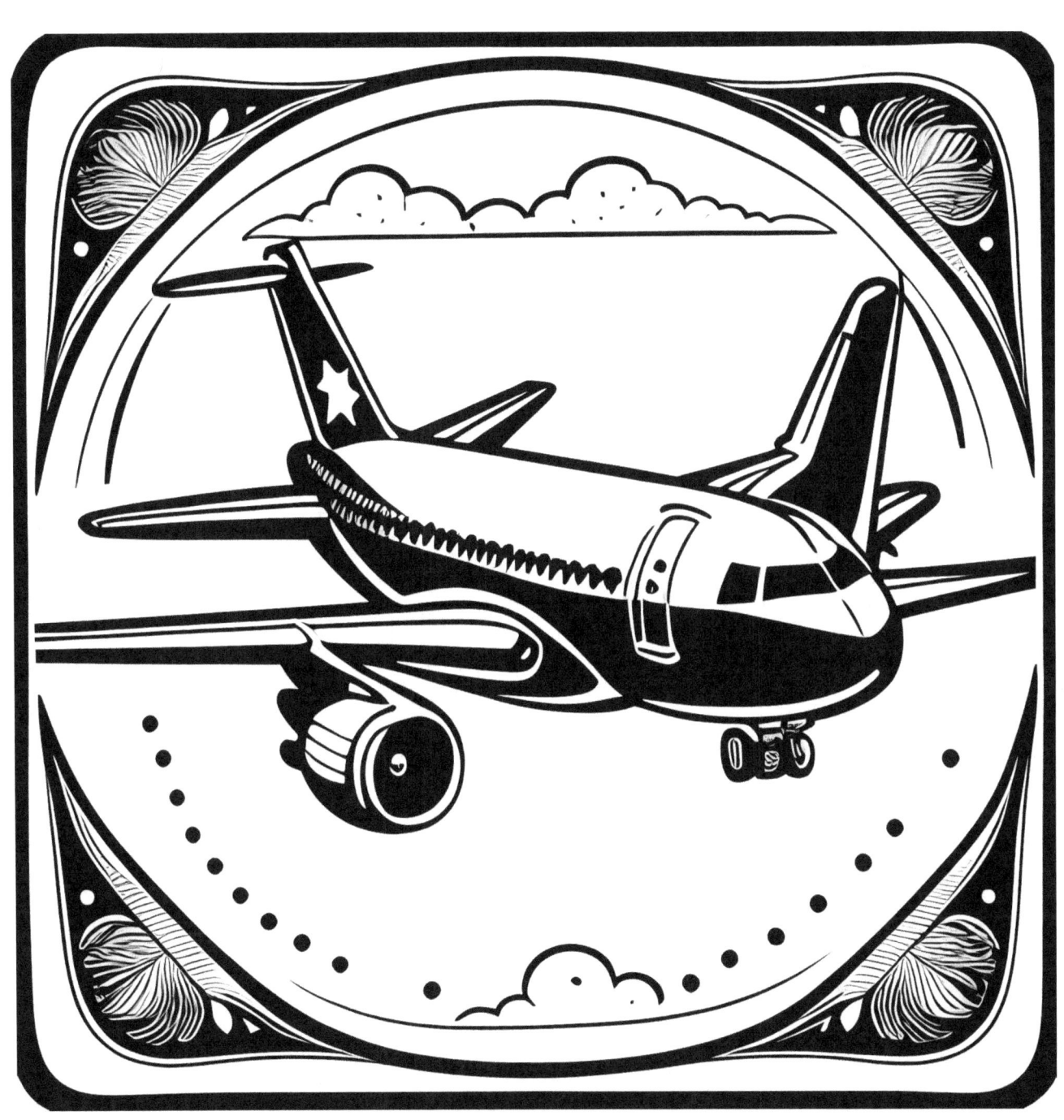

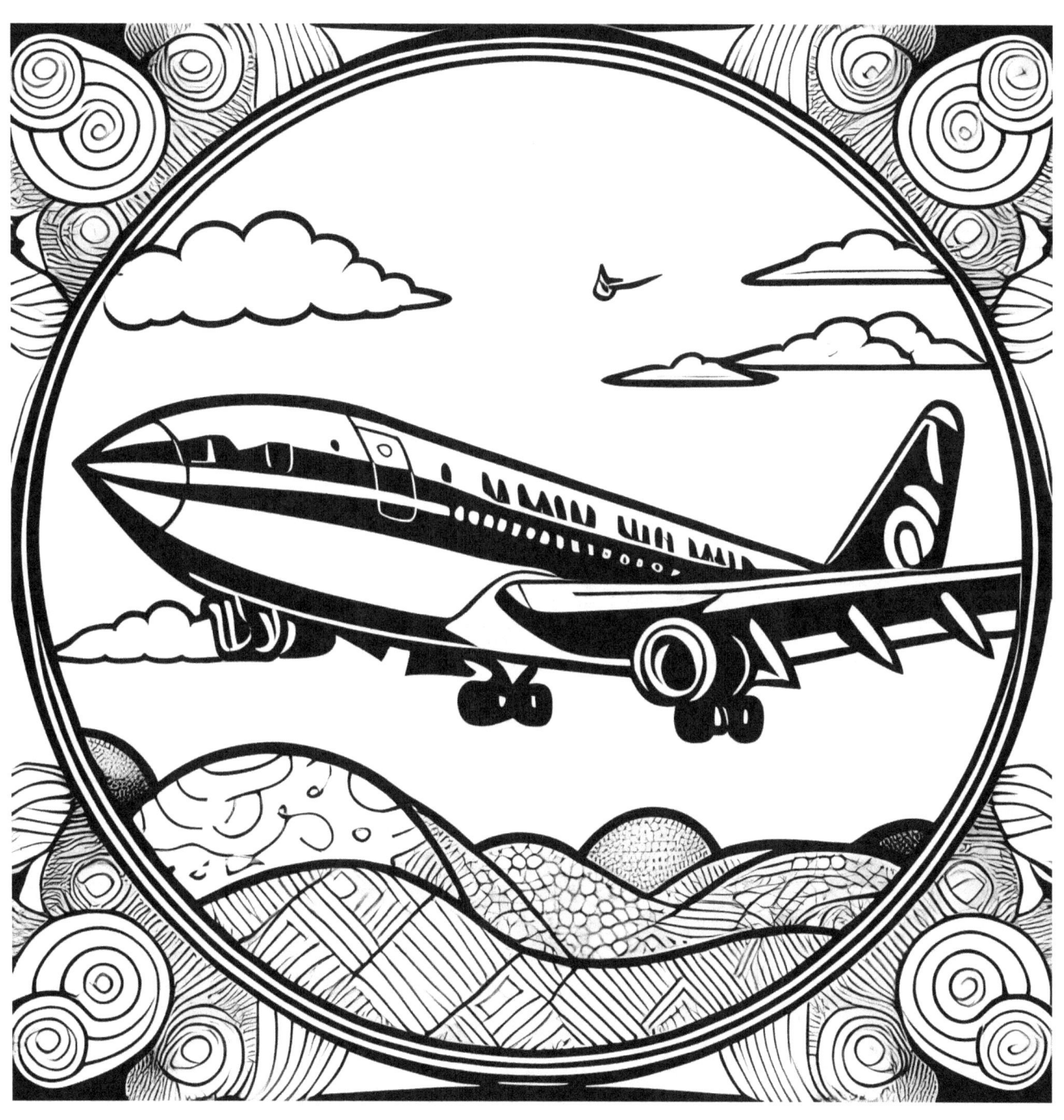

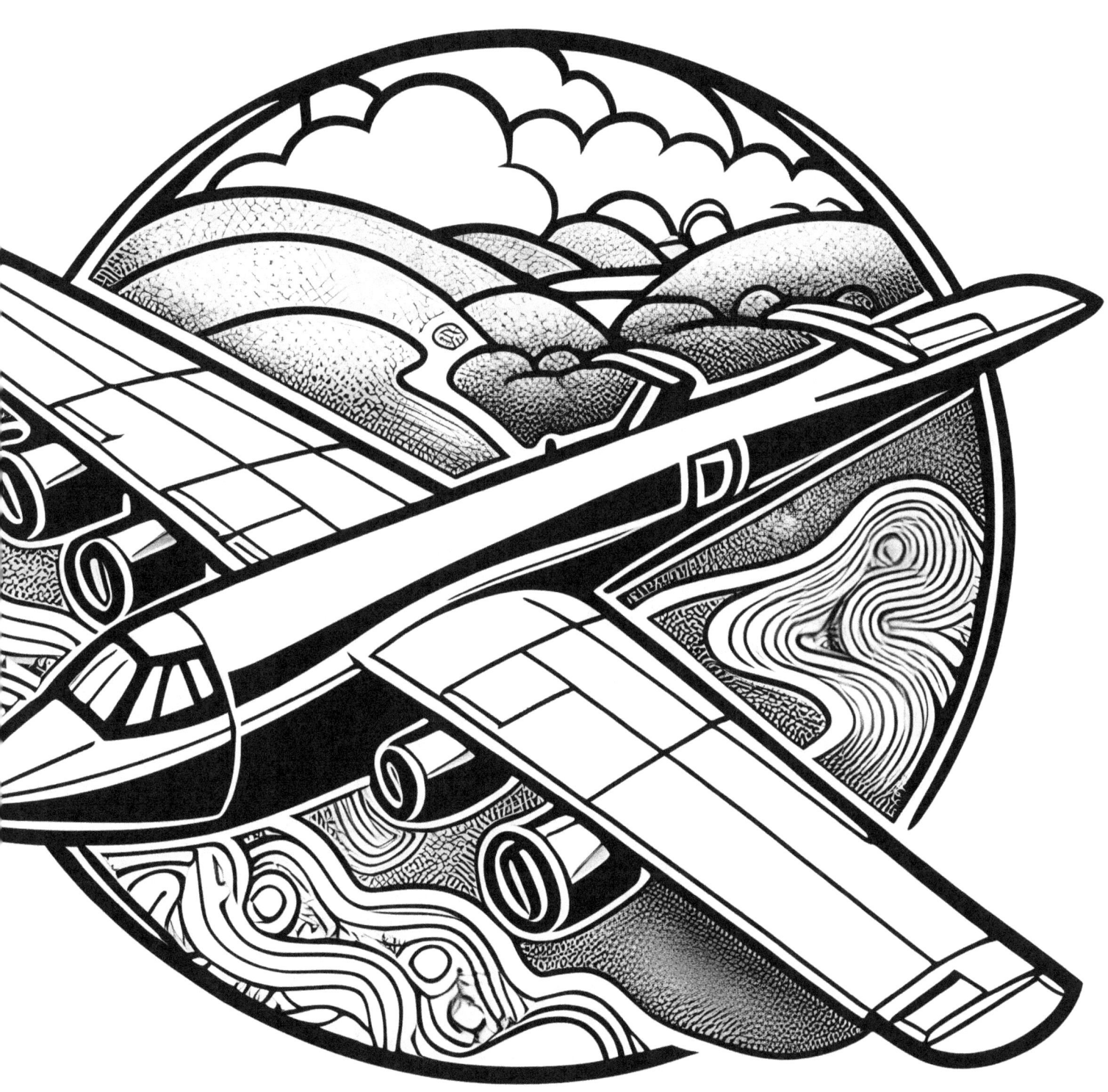

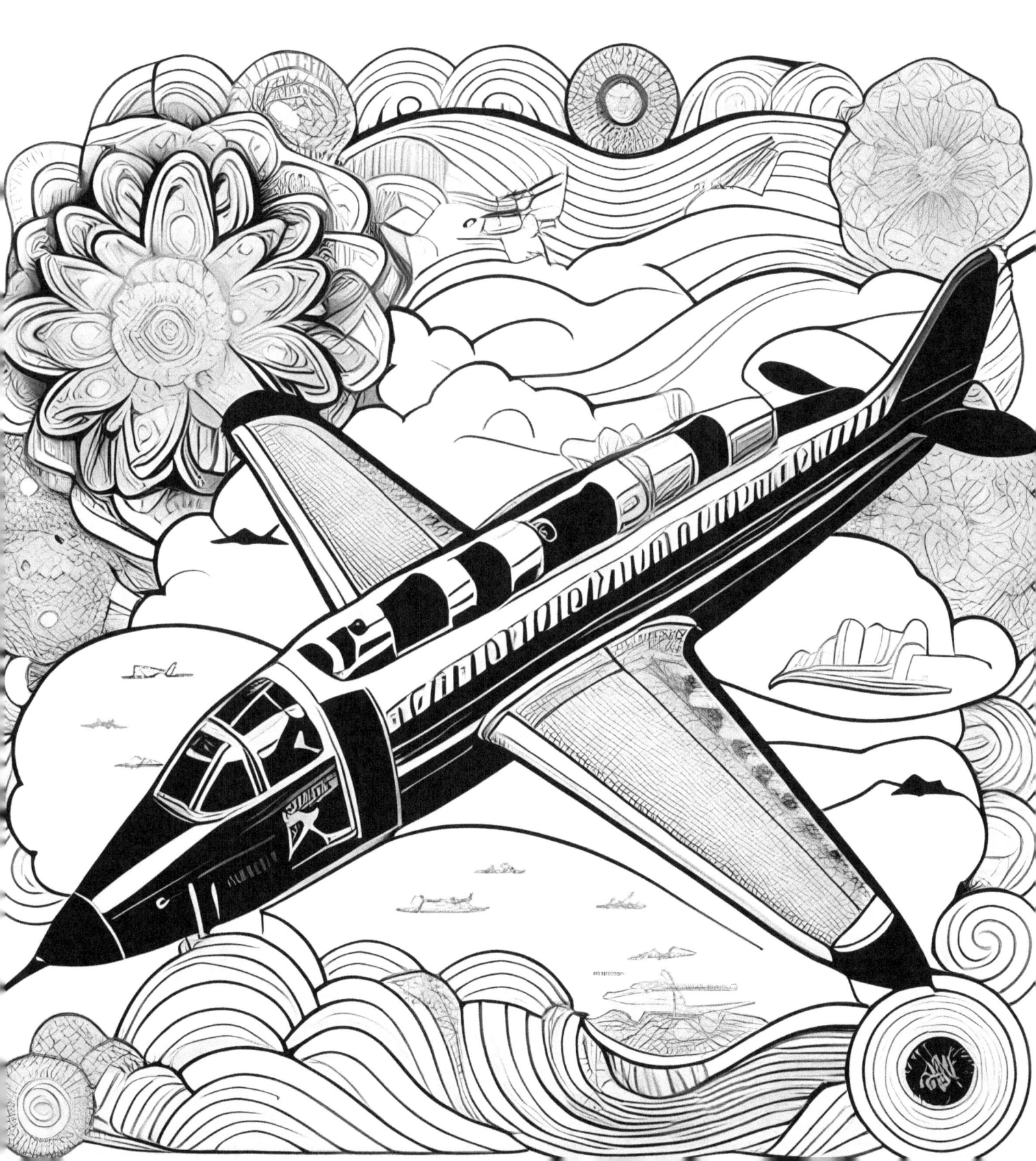

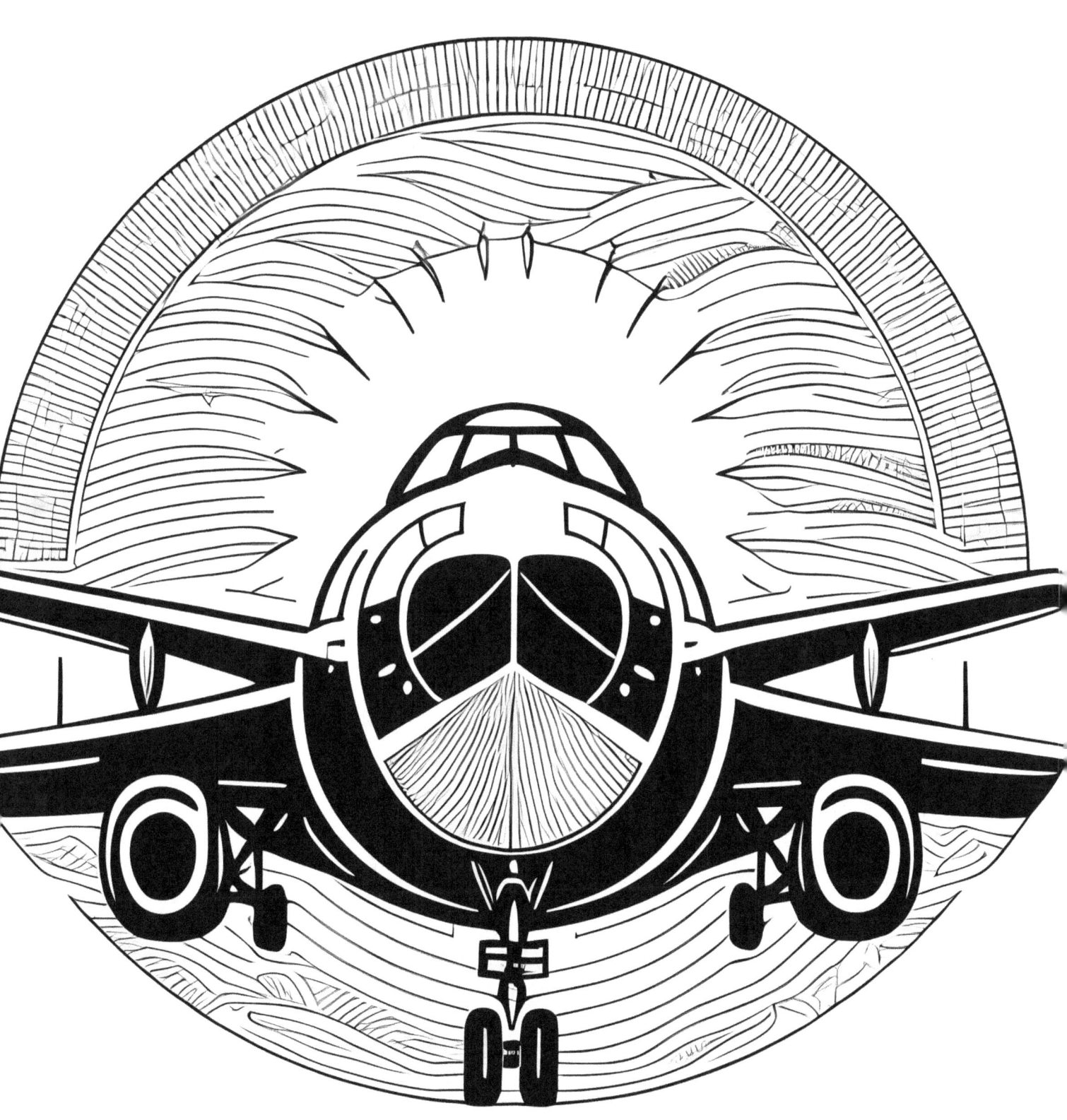

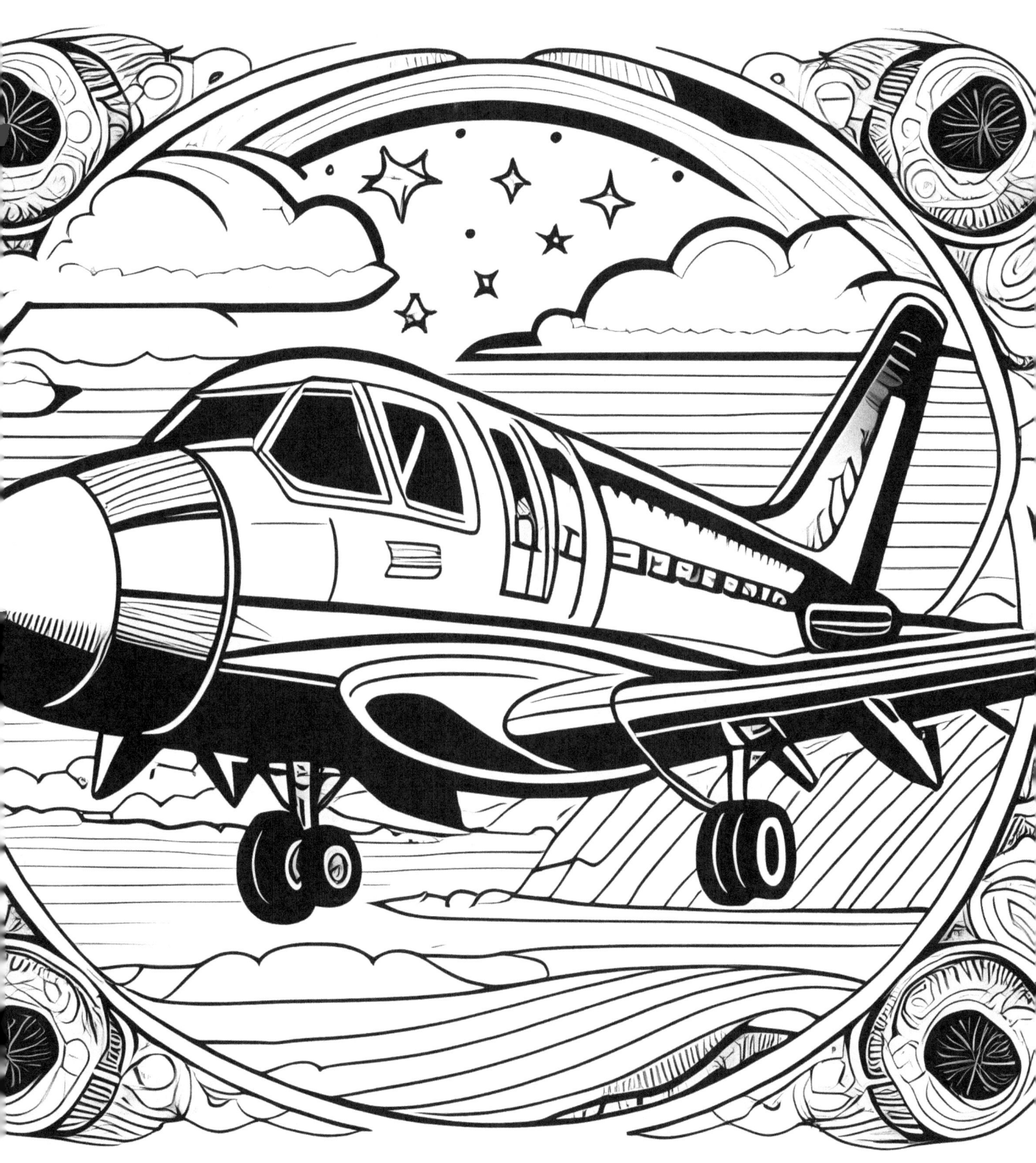

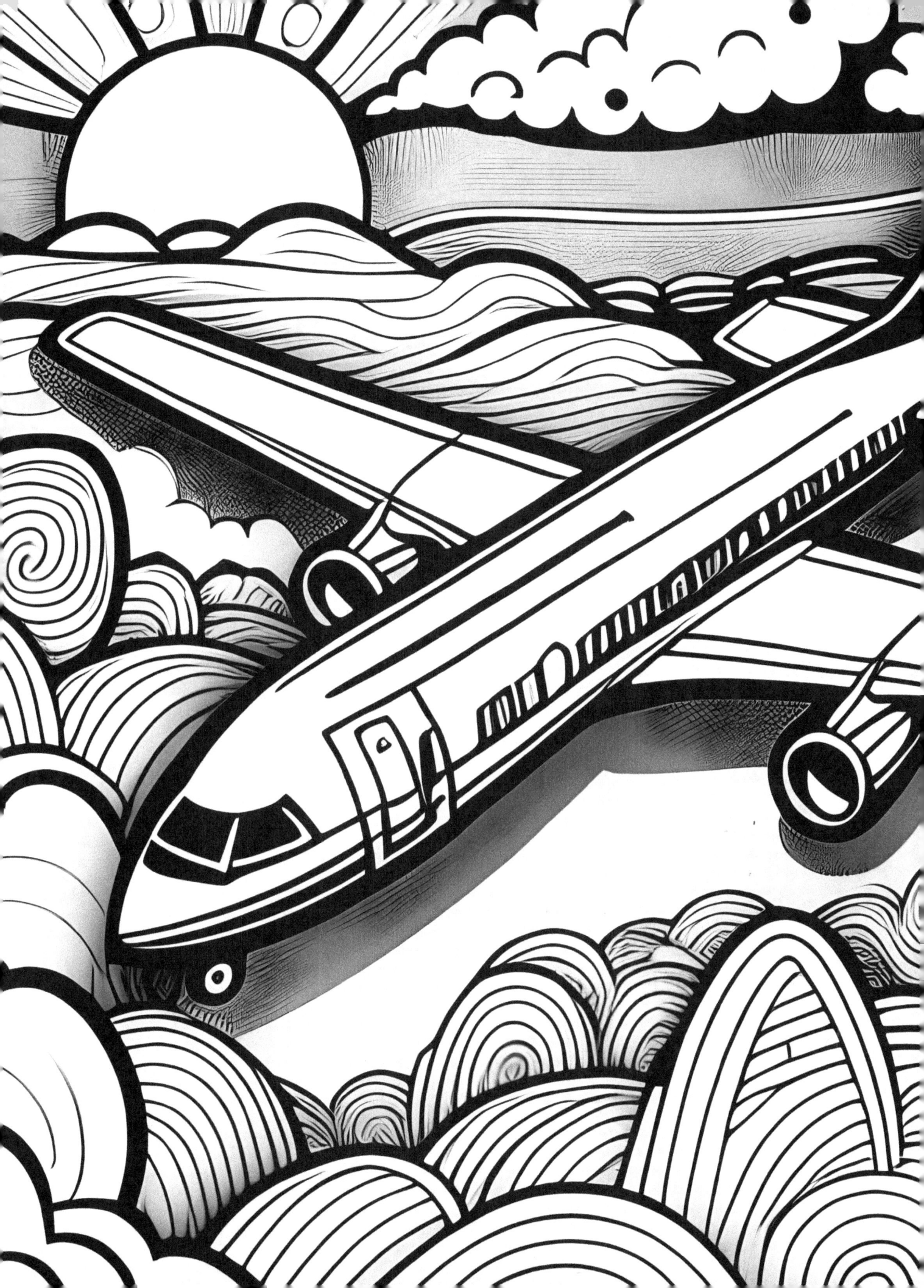

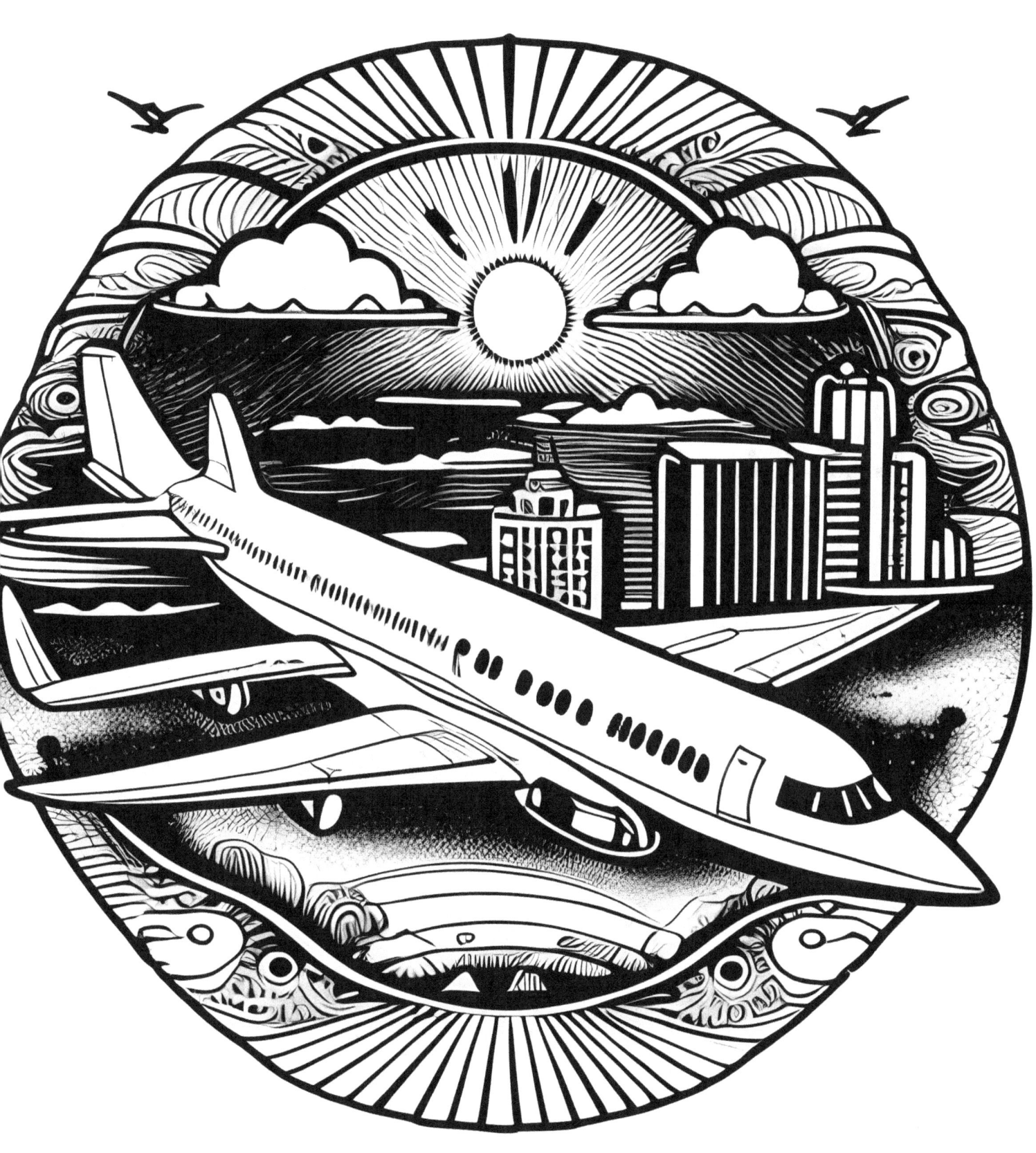

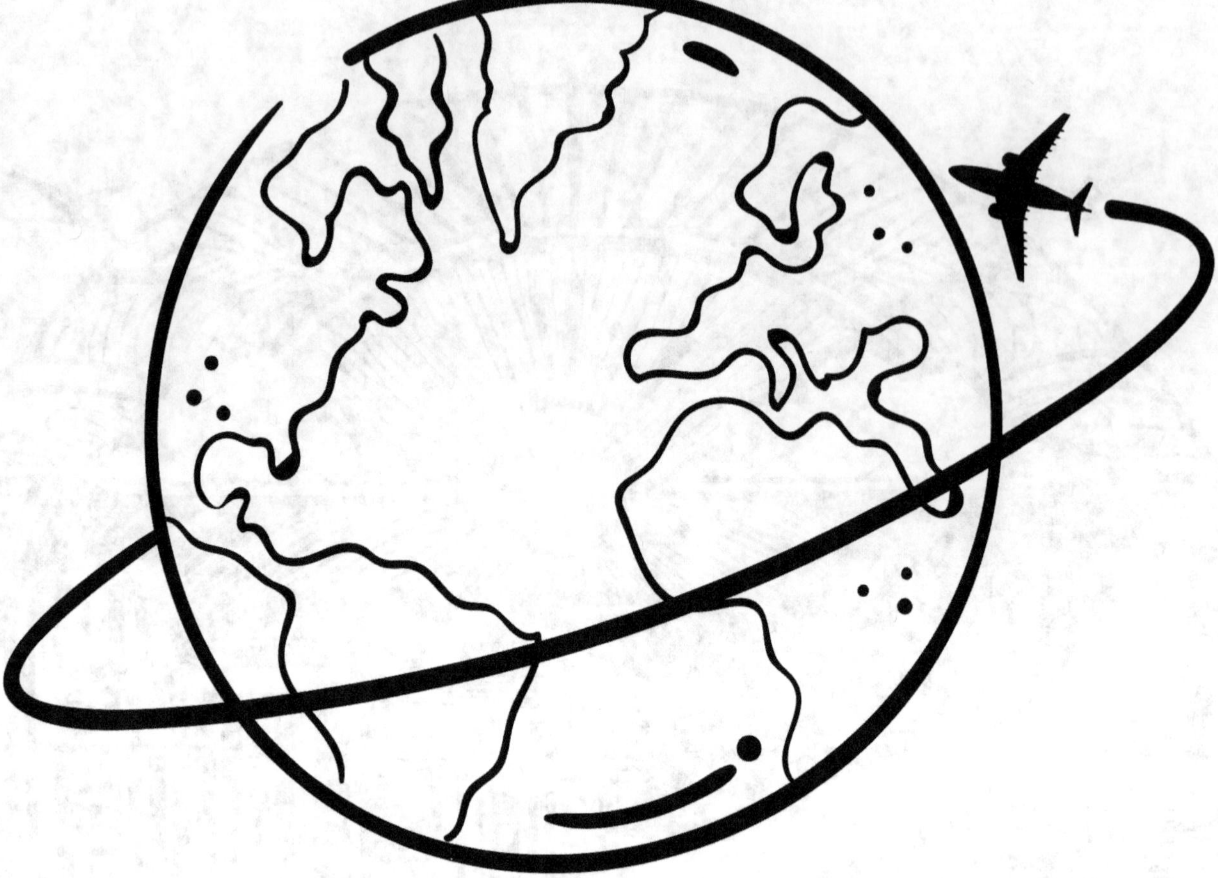

Thank you for purchasing this book, please leave a review!

★★★★★

NOEMIN.

www.ingramcontent.com/pod-product-compliance
Lightning Source LLC
Chambersburg PA
CBHW062217220526
45471CB00009B/3240